JULIAN COSTLEY

HOW TO: USE CROWDFUNDING

bluebird
books for life

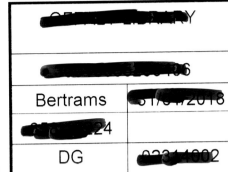

First published 2017 by Bluebird
an imprint of Pan Macmillan
20 New Wharf Road, London N1 9RR
Associated companies throughout the world
www.panmacmillan.com

ISBN 978-1-5098-1451-0

Visit **www.panmacmillan.com** to read more about all our books
and to buy them. You will also find features, author interviews and
news of any author events, and you can sign up for e-newsletters
so that you're always first to hear about our new releases.

HOW TO: USE CROWDFUNDING

Julian Costley, with over forty years' experience of starting companies, raising funds, and making considerable money for his shareholders, is an entrepreneur's entrepreneur, keen to help others achieve their dreams. He describes himself as a poacher turned gamekeeper, having held senior roles at Reuters, BSkyB, France Telecom, and E*TRADE UK before switching to become an angel investor successfully securing start-up capital from investors large and small.

how to: ACADEMY launched in September 2013. Since then it has organized over 400 talks and seminars on Business, Lifestyle, and Science & Technology, which have been attended by 40,000 people. The aim of the series is to anticipate the needs of the reader by providing clarity, precision and know-how in an increasingly complex world.

Contents

Introduction 1

1: What is Crowdfunding? 7

2: Is Crowdfunding for Me? 16

3: How to Get Ready 35

4: How to Make a Financial Plan 49

5: How to Tell Your Story 63

6: Planning the Campaign 86

7: Going Live! 103

8: Hitting (or Missing) Your Target 121

9: Conclusion: Secrets of Success 130

Further Reading 137

Appendix I – Setting up a company 142

Appendix II – Choosing a domain name 147

Appendix III – Using the brand pyramid to define your brand 155

Appendix IV – EIS and SEIS 161

Appendix V – Tips on shaping a board 167

Appendix VI – Top 20 factors that maximize shareholder value 171

Index 178

Introduction

So you want to raise funds?

Whether you've bought this book because you are a budding entrepreneur with a brilliant idea that needs funding, or because it looks like the perfect motivation for someone you know, then congratulations! You, or they, are already on the path to success.

What follows is a practical guide for individuals, companies and other organizations contemplating a crowdfunding campaign. It will also encompass crowdlending – the process by which two or more individuals lend funds to a company in return for financial interest payments.

Crowdfunding is defined as a process by which a proposition is offered by a company, either directly or via a Crowdfunding Service Company (CSC), to two or more individuals (the 'crowd'). The crowd participates in the process by agreeing to subscribe to shares in the company or pledge funds in return for rewards, discounts on the company's services or products, or for simple recognition of their donations towards the company's crowdfunding campaign goal.

Be warned. Crowdfunding is not for the faint-hearted. As on a mountain climb, you're going to need more than a route map. The journey requires meticulous planning, the right support team, equipment, know-how and fitness. But above all, it requires a steely determination to continue despite the hazards, the frustrations, the inefficiencies of others and the inevitable feelings of 'is all this worth it?'

The good news is that well-organized campaigns, based on credible business or project plans and run by enthusiastic management, have a high probability of getting the money needed.

Funding-by-the-crowd is not a new idea. We've all seen those painted thermometers on the sides of churches, showing the progress towards raising the target needed to repair the roof.

Crowdfunding on the internet first gained popular and mainstream use in the arts and music communities. The first instance of crowdfunding as we now know it was in 1997, when fans underwrote an entire US tour for the British rock group Carillion, raising US$60,000 in donations by means of a fan-based internet campaign.

Crowdfunding gained traction after the launch of Artist-Share, IndieGoGo (both 2008), Kickstarter (2009) and Microventures (2010). However, Sellaband, started in 2006 as a music-focused platform, initially controlled the crowdfunding market.

The highest reported funding by a crowdfunded project at the time of writing is for *Star Citizen*, a space trading and combat online video game being developed by Chris Roberts and Cloud Imperium Games. As of 21 November 2016, they claim to have raised over US$133,000,000, beating the previous record of US$10,266,844, set by Pebble Watch.

The projects seeking crowdfunding now encompass pretty much everything, from charities to product prototypes, theatrical events to significant businesses. Although individual investments can range from £10 to £25,000, the average for more serious fundraises is around £250.

So, it's an active marketplace, with ever more potential investors. The time might be right to unleash your passion and get cracking!

About this book – how to use it to run a successful fundraising campaign

This book is a step-by-step guide to setting up, running and concluding your crowdfunding campaign. We'll begin by examining the types of funding available to you out there, then I'll throw you a bunch of facts to show what's possible. In chapter 2 I'll share a case study that will give an idea of what a crowdfunding campaign looks like in practice. Then come a few questions that will challenge you and your project's suitability for funding.

Next is a major section on getting investment-ready, which essentially covers everything your future investor will want to know – the idea, the team, the financial projections, and so on. I've included advice on how to value your business, how to decide the amount of funding you need, and thus how much of your company shares, or equity, you're prepared to sell to the new investors.

Then I'll help you choose the right crowdfunding company, guide you on working with them to prepare the online campaign and what to do once the campaign has started. Lastly, there are some reassuring tips on dealing with the end of the whole process, whether you've reached your target or, just as importantly, your campaign has failed.

The market is moving so fast that a book like this can only

provide a snapshot of what's going on. My advice is to set up a Google Alert (free at the time of writing) and use 'crowdfunding' and 'angel investing' keywords. You'll be inundated with up to twenty emails a day, but pan for gold and you'll find some nuggets of new and helpful information!

Be positive, be determined

Great ideas and great management have a good chance of getting funded. The difference between success and failure in any endeavour is often that final spur of effort. Telling yourself 'I can do this.' Let me give you a great example of what happens if you push yourself that bit further.

Marquis Jet co-founder Jesse Itzler learned about the 40 per cent rule from a US Navy SEAL, whom he first met during a hundred-mile race (the SEAL was running solo, while Itzler was part of a relay team). The SEAL completed the race despite breaking all the small bones in his feet and suffering kidney damage. Itzler was so impressed with this mental toughness that he hired the SEAL to live with him and his family for a month to help them shake up their routine and live more purposefully.[1]

On one occasion when the SEAL was living with them, he challenged Jesse by asking how many press-ups he could do. After Jesse did eight, the SEAL suggested he rested and try again. On each subsequent attempt, as Jesse became increasingly tired, the number fell from eight to six, to three, and then no more. The SEAL insisted he was not leaving until 100 had been reached. Jesse thought that this would take quite some time! But he did it; one press-up at a time.

Jesse said he'd learned an important lesson – we're all so much more capable than we think.

According to the SEAL, the 40 per cent rule states that when your mind tells you that you can't do any more, you're really only about 40 per cent done. This is why marathon runners so often 'hit the wall' somewhere in the middle of their race but are still able to finish.

I've been very fortunate to have what my mother referred to as a 'sunny disposition', so I'm naturally a positive person. And I know from having run many companies that when people lack motivation, the simplest of tasks are hard to get done.

Determination is the key, and there are three simple processes you can undertake that will increase your determination:

1. Gather a group of friends or business colleagues – independent people whose honest opinion you'll take. Tell them about your fundraising plans and ask them if they will support you and provide the occasional motivating chat throughout the process.
2. Find a mentor. Mentored SME businesses are twice as likely to succeed than non-mentored businesses according to research.[2] He or she has got be someone who's 'been there and done it'. Not necessarily older than you, or even in the same sector. Just a grown-up with a tough but empathetic character, who will keep asking you the critical questions and keep you on track.
3. Create a plan. We'll cover this later in the book, but for now the important point is that a plan is like a GPS road map – it gives clear directions and an estimated time of arrival.

1:

WHAT IS CROWDFUNDING?

Equity crowdfunding, crowdlending and rewards crowdfunding explained

There are essentially three types of crowdfunding:

1: Equity crowdfunding

Equity crowdfunding is where you 'sell' shares in your company to an investor. They are not lending you the money, nor are you selling them any of your products or services. Here is a practical example. You want to raise £100,000 and you have formed a company with 100,000 shares. You own all the shares, so you own 100 per cent of the equity. You decide to let the new investor have 20 per cent of the shares in the company after they've put in the money. So, if their £100,000 represents 20 per cent of the company it means that, after their investment, the company is worth £500,000. Or £400,000 before. If there were 100,000 shares before and they were, together, worth £400,000, then each share is worth £4. To enable the investor to buy shares you will have to 'issue' more. At £4 per share you'll need to issue 25,000 new shares (£100,000 divided by £4). There were 100,000 shares before the investment and you've issued 25,000 more. So there are now 125,000 shares. Your new investor has 25,000 of the 125,000 which of course is 20 per cent of the 'equity'.

Don't be put off by the complications of the maths or even the logic. I use my trusted lawyer to check the maths whenever I raise funds. But, as you'll read in later chapters, it is essential to master the basic structures of equity.

Across the whole of the UK crowdfunding market, most crowdfunding companies will do equity crowdfunding. But not all of them have a large or relevant 'crowd' – meaning the members of the public who have signed up on their websites as potential investors. There are generalists and there are firms dedicated to specializations – like theatre projects or app software – but the size and relevance of their database of potential investors is not the only factor you'll take into consideration, as discussed later.

2: Crowdlending (or debt crowdfunding)

Debt crowdfunding, as the name suggests, is raising money given to you as a loan. You'll have read about payday loans, run by companies such as Zopa, RateSetter, LendInvest, Madiston and Wellesley & Co. This is known as peer-to-peer lending. This means that the crowdfunding company orchestrates the online connection between someone wanting a personal loan and one or more individuals prepared to lend it to them for a pre-determined interest over a fixed time period.

Although the characteristics of debt crowdfunding or crowdlending in the business markets are similar, they are run far more like a modern-day banking loan. The market leaders in this space are Funding Circle, Funding Knight, and Thin Cats.

The main difference between consumer peer-to-peer and business debt crowdfunding is that, like the banks, the crowdfunding company will want to see evidence that your company has the means of paying the loan back. They will want to see a minimum of three years of trading history, a strong balance sheet (meaning, among other things, that you've not already borrowed substantially elsewhere) and almost certainly a trading history which shows that your profits, or at least your cash flow, are high enough in previous years to afford the repayments on the loan.

For this reason, debt crowdfunding is not really suitable for very early-stage businesses. But it's worth becoming familiar with the benefits of debt crowdfunding, as it makes sense, when you can afford it, to borrow money in a sensible balance to selling shares. Why? If – as in the example above – your company is worth £500,000 now but worth £10,000,000 in five years' time, your investor who bought 20 per cent will own 20 per cent of that £10,000,000. A cool £2m. But if they had *lent* you the money, even at a very high interest rate of 10 per cent, that £100,000 would only have grown to £146,100 (less, if you had paid back the loan in stages). Obviously, paying back £146,100 is a bargain in relation to letting them keep £2m. This is why most companies, as they grow and get stronger, build debt into their funding. And you'll want to do the same.

What's good about this form of debt is that the crowdfunding companies have knocked the spots off clearing banks in terms of speed of decision and processing of the applications. And because their online marketplaces allow the interest rate to 'float' competitively to the right level of investor acceptance, companies with a low-risk need for funds often get attractive borrowing rates. Typical rates are a little higher than a clearing bank but that reflects the fact that crowdlenders will lend on your trading history, prospects and cash flow, whereas a bank will often ask for security in terms of a personal guarantee or a 'charge' on an asset. The difference of approach gets converted into a small increase in interest rate – often referred to as a 'risk premium'. The key is to have a reason for the money. Increased need for additional working capital resulting from a large customer order will be looked on favourably.

3: Rewards (or perks) crowdfunding

Rewards or perks crowdfunding works like this. Imagine you are raising funds to start an online ticketing agency via a new app – concerts, events, etc. It's going to be a subscription service costing £100 per annum, but the subscribers get discounts on cinema, concerts, live events, etc. which you've negotiated with the event organizers. You only need a small amount – say £50,000 to develop the software. Your company may be of very little value at the moment, with no trading history. Even if you valued the company at £100,000, raising £50,000 in equity would mean 'giving away' (as equity investing is often referred to) 33 per cent of your company. Pre-money valuation (the valuation before investor money goes in) is £100,000 and post money is £150,000. So the new investor gets 50/150, or 33 per cent of the company. Too much!

What rewards crowdfunding allows you to do is pre-sell your investors the subscription service you will be providing. You might say to investors, 'pledge £100 and you'll get the service free for life'. To get £50,000, you'll only need 500 people in the 'crowd' to take your subscription offer. You use the £50,000 you get to build the app, and you launch. Assuming the business does well and you end up, after the first year, selling 2,000 membership subscriptions at full price, your gross income is £200,000. And you don't owe a penny to your 'investors'. In fact, the dilutive effect on your business at the end of year one is only 25 per cent – meaning 50 out of every 200 subscribers are creating no revenue. As the business grows, that core of early adopters will also become a progressively smaller part of your customer mix.

Artlyst Limited, the online news, reviews, and listings guide to the contemporary art scene in London, ran an awards campaign. The company successfully raised £40,000 for a new web front end, and did it through rewards crowdfunding with the crowdfunding company CrowdShed. Artlyst, with CrowdShed's support, was able to create an innovative list of rewards that ranged from dinner with the editor through to a day-long personal guided tour of the annual Frieze exhibition, held in October each year.

As this shows, rewards work well when you have something tangible to offer – such as the opportunity to buy a product at a discount when it becomes available, or to exchange something of little cost to you for money from an investor who regards that reward as very good value. There have been many examples recently of product prototypes being funded this way, such as camera-carrying drones.

One cautionary word. The money investors' pledge for a reward campaign is non-refundable. They get the reward but they don't get any shares in your company. For that reason, investors can't claim investor's tax relief under the UK government's EIS (Enterprise Investment Scheme). See Appendix IV for how that works. This means that if your subscription service company fails, the investors will no longer get the free subscription each year or the discounts that the subscription brought them, whereas if they invested into your company, bought shares, and subsequently your company failed, they could claim tax relief, turning an initial investment into a smaller loss.

Example:

Investment = £10,000

Income Tax relief = £3,000 (as a reduction in your income tax bill)

At risk capital = £7,000

Loss relief on at risk capital @ 45 per cent = £3,150

Your actual loss = £3,850 (£10,000 – [£3,000 + £3,150])

Tip: Almost every successful equity campaign is now a hybrid of equity and rewards crowdfunding. It's always wise to think of how to sweeten the deal with your investors by offering them something extra in addition to the shares they're getting. It can be as simple as mailing out a low-cost product from your range, such as a sports water bottle, as Sundried did when I recently invested in them.

What's the difference between crowdfunding and angel investing?

Angel investing is all about attracting interest and commitment from individual private investors.

Who are they? These are private individuals who make investments directly into (mostly) early-stage companies. In the UK, they would typically invest from £10,000 to £100,000 in any one company.

These are their characteristics:

- They have run and sold businesses, giving rise to

wealth that is put into differing investment assets, creating a balance of risk. These might be property and fixed-interest securities representing the low-risk part of their portfolio, and high-risk investment including leveraged securities like options, spread betting or CFDs (contracts for difference), and investments in start-up or early-stage companies.

- They are very clued-up and have the same access as you do to the research and market data on the internet, so they are knowledgeable and challenging.

- They tend to invest in industry sectors where they have spent much of their career.

- They like to invest in groups – this can be an informal grouping of similarly wealthy friends or colleagues, or it can be via angel investment clubs.

- They don't always invest in UK companies, but investing outside the UK usually means they would lose the benefits of EIS.

- They don't always demand to come on your board of directors, but that's a function of a) the time they have available for you, b) the significance of their investment (often shareholders who invest over 10 per cent of the equity of a company would expect a directorship to be automatic) and c) whether you've offered them an augmented role, such as chairperson, or an interim executive function – like part-time Chief Financial Officer.

- If they come on the board or play any sort of active support role, they may expect fees. Start-up companies seeking around £250,000 of funds will probably have to pay around £15,000 per annum for an active non-executive director. But angels are usually happy to either defer that fee and roll it up for later payment, take a few more shares instead, take options, or simply waive the fees for the first year or until the company can afford to pay. Expect to pay up to £25,000 per annum once your company is profitable and growing.

- Angels are invariably experienced business people, and often older than the typical entrepreneur. As such, they tend to be good mentors. It's a wise entrepreneur who chooses an angel for their guidance skills as much as for their money, industry know-how and connections.

- Ideally, you want a good spread of angel investors with an average of £20,000 from each, so that your shareholder group is manageable. Six to ten angel investors is fine. And they can't all come on the board – so don't promise anything to any of them until you have a complete picture of how your angel part of the pre-funding shapes up.

- Lastly, be careful not to allow any one investor to take too large a share. On the one hand, it's very encouraging and should in theory speed up the process, but on the other hand shareholders with 10 per cent or more can adversely influence board decisions, and if they get more than 25 per cent their shareholder rights increase and they are in a powerful position (see Appendix V – Tips on shaping a board).

Key tip: As we'll learn later, a successful crowdfunding campaign needs pre-funding. This means that before your fundraising campaign goes live on the website, you'll be expected to find up to 33 per cent of the total yourself. So, a £180,000 campaign will need you to go and find around £60,000 beforehand. Learning how to approach individuals – for which, read angel investors – with a strong investment proposition and securing their commitment is going to be required, even if it's a crowdfunding campaign.

2:

IS CROWDFUNDING FOR ME?

Ah! That's the key question! There are a number of alternative ways to raise money for your business or project. In the previous chapter, I outlined the three main types of crowdfunding. But your choice is wider. The full list of funding options is below, and I'll give you guidance as to when you might consider each before examining the costs of crowdfunding.

— Friends and Family

— Angel investors

— Equity crowdfunding

— Rewards crowdfunding

— Crowdlending

— Customer funding

— Bank debt

— Grants and matched funds

— R & D tax credits

Friends and Family

Friends and Family (F&F) is an expression used in venture capital and early-stage fundraising. It's usually for when your idea or business is very new, perhaps too new to have credibility with professional investors. This type of funding is when you might be raising no more than £50,000 to do some research, or build a prototype, or to write software, or get a simple website built. It might be that you know an investor already and they may be prepared to put some very early-stage money into the business and provide some mentoring. At this stage, you'd have to show that you were prepared to put a lot of your time into the business, as well as some of your own money. Often, entrepreneurs will raise F&F funding while still employed in their 'day job' and moonlight on the new project until it's ready for more substantial funding.

Angel investors

These are individuals who invest in early-stage businesses for a number of reasons. Ultimately to make a return on their investment, but also for the fun of getting involved in helping a company grow to the next stage. If you think you need between £100,000 and £250,000, this could be a suitable alternative to crowdfunding. An individual angel might invest between £10,000 and £50,000.

I would go for 100 per cent angel funding if your idea or business is more B2B (Business to Business) rather than consumer focused. This is for two reasons. First, the crowdfunding 'crowd' can better identify with a product they might want to actually buy themselves – like a new camera, a craft beer, clothing, or perhaps a consumer service like a holiday company. They struggle with complex propositions such as security algorithms, or software services to corporations. Second, angel investors nowadays are nearly always successful entrepreneurs in their own right and have 'cashed out' on one or more sales of their businesses. This means that they will have both sector and operational expertise, and they'll have the time to focus on your business, because it's worth their time to do so if they've invested a significant sum – as opposed to a crowdfunder who may only have invested £20.

Having said all that, you will almost certainly have to attract one or more angel investors as part of a crowdfunding campaign. This is because, as mentioned above and discussed in more detail later, a crowdfunding campaign has to be 'primed' with a minimum of 33 per cent of your target to have enough momentum to attract the crowd. In reality, finding and persuading angel investors to invest is not really an 'alternative' if you're going to run a crowdfunding campaign – you're going to need them.

Equity crowdfunding

This is when you give investors a share of your company in return for them buying shares. It works well in situations where there is the expectation that your business could grow to something substantial. This is because the crowdfunder will be looking to make many times their investment in return. Why? Because investing in early-stage businesses is a far higher risk than putting money on deposit with a bank or building society. You'll need to be a business that could scale.

Rewards crowdfunding

This, you'll recall, is where the 'crowd' are given tangible rewards, either as a bonus to their equity investment or as the only benefit. For example, you might offer discounted tickets to a stage production you are writing and producing in return for giving you money. The tickets might be priced at £50 for public sale, but you let the crowd have them for £15 each. The proposition is that they will get that reward of the saving only when your production goes live. If it never does, then they lose their money. You might like to consider this type of crowdfunding if it doesn't make sense to have hundreds of small investors in your small business – because of the complication and drain on your time looking after them.

But combining rewards with a conventional equity campaign can be very effective, and could be the offer that tips an investor over the edge to start backing you!

Crowdlending

As discussed in chapter 1, crowdlending is only really possible if you have a trading track record. It's essentially old-style bank loans but with the new twist of the consumer bidding for your debt. So, because it has a credit risk associated with it, crowdlending tends to be provided by established companies with professional teams assessing your business and balance sheet. For that reason, they are very cautious and risk averse – they don't want the crowdlenders out there to be offered risky debt. The good news is that they work much faster than the banks used to, and the interest you'll pay tends to 'float' to accommodate the level of risk perceived by the lending crowd.

Customer funding

One of the least publicized methods among the start-up community is using customer cash to fund your business. Yet it can be more effective in long-term shareholder value than bank debt or investor equity.

Not all companies can take advantage of the various ways in which customer funding can be achieved. I recall launching a TV channel on BSB (British Satellite Broadcasting – later to become BSkyB and now Sky). Even before the first revenues were obtainable from our satellite channel subscribers, I had to hire a team, design and pay for the studio set, hire and pre-pay for on-screen talent and expert guests, and produce a number of programmes in advance, so that we had something to broadcast when we went on air. Oh, and I had to pay for a large channel launch party to attract all the thirsty journalists. Not a model that lent itself to securing money in advance from my customers.

Contrast this with Airbnb. Launched in 2007 by two design school graduates, it used pre-payments by customers booking accommodation to fund the early stages of the company. Once they had 'traction', traditional venture capital funds were available at a very attractive valuation. By 2012, they had raised $120m and were valued at more than $1bn.

The business model allowed them to use customer money to develop the company without the compromises often associated with external funding – such as shareholder influence on strategy. They had a free hand and were successful, as entrepreneurs often are when doing things 'their way'.

Getting cash in before you have to spend that cash is often referred to as 'negative working capital'. It's a well-trodden path for many service industries. If a law firm charges you a retainer before the work is executed, then they are customer funding.

Google encourages its online customers to spend on AdWords before they have to pay Google for the service. In that way, its customers (it is hoped) can generate revenue in excess of the cost of the advertising that brought in the business. Even small firms can be granted £1m of credit to adopt this sales tactic.

The beauty of customer pre-payment is that it obviates many of the problems associated, say, with bank loans, where security is often required in the form of a charge on assets or personal guarantees.

John Mullins, Associate Professor of Management Practice in Marketing and Entrepreneurship at London Business School, has identified five distinct customer-funded models, which he published in the *Harvard Business Review* in 2013.[3] I've outlined these below.

1. The matchmaker model

This is where a company sits in between buyers and sellers and connects them. Very little working capital is required, as the company holds no inventory and has no operating costs relating to delivery. Think of estate agents, and organizations like eBay, Expedia, etc.

This model works well in an economy where there are underutilized assets. A good example is www.boatbookings.com, founded and run by the very capable Tom Virden, one of the top team and early senior executives at www.lastminute.com. Tom identified that there were hundreds of thousands of yachts around the world that were hardly used by their owners. Hey presto! An Airbnb model for the boat market.

2. The deposit model

This is where the customer pays in advance in the form of a deposit. The travel industry operate extensively on this basis, as do all sectors where the organizations down the food chain – such as hotels – need assurance that the agent has the means of fulfilling the booking obligation. Airlines have been taking our ticket purchase money well in advance for decades!

3. The subscription model

Fairly obviously, most subscription businesses seek payment in advance. If you've been encouraged to opt for an annual subscription for, say, car insurance, you're unwittingly providing a major source of working capital to the insurer, since their operating costs will be evenly spread throughout the year of the subscription. So attractive is this, that insurers can offer a 5 per cent discount or even more, and still be far better off than would be the case with monthly payments.

The only real advance cost for them is 'customer acquisition', or 'selling costs'. Those subscriptions need to be sold somehow. But the cash from the early subscriptions can be used to pay the sales staff and the external marketing costs – so the model works all round.

4. The standardize-and-resell model

Many years ago, I worked for the venerable Exchange Telegraph Company. Their heritage dated back about as far as the Reuters News agency, with its initial use of pigeons to deliver critical messages before electronic means were invented.

I worked in the more modern Extel Computing subsidiary, which provided complex share price data to asset management companies, enabling them to value their portfolios. There was always a stream of special requests by the customers for changes to our software. Often the changes were expensive to develop but the customer could rarely be charged the full cost of the work, and for a while we lost money each time we developed the new features. So, my talented CEO, Mike Warburg, cleverly took the new features round to all our similar customers and sold the enhancement to all of them. He not only covered the cost, but also made an additional profit, while at the same time impressing all the customers with the constant product innovations.

The model only worked by standardizing the offering so it could be offered to many customers in a common format.

The strategy of securing a contract to create something for one customer and then reselling a variant of that product on a wider scale can work well for small firms. The perfect example is Microsoft's operating system – it was written for IBM, but became a world standard!

5. The scarcity model

This model has worked well for retailers. Companies like the Spanish group Zara, the French chain Monoprix and

Swedish giants H&M have made a policy of running up to twenty-six 'seasons' a year. They might sell items for only two weeks at a time at any one store, and in so doing set a pattern with consumers – you should buy when you see something you like, because it might not be there when you next visit the store. This 'brings forward' customer cash, and yet the suppliers are all on extended invoice payment periods. This strategy supports both the cash flow and the brand positioning, since the perception is that the stores are always up to date with the very latest fashions.

Bank debt

Although it seems old-fashioned now, getting an overdraft from a clearing bank makes sense. You'll need to offer some collateral or security, but if you're in a position to do so then it's a quick process. Security may take the form of a charge on an asset – like a mortgage or simply a personal guarantee. Interest rates will be high but if it is used in conjunction with some F&F funding then this makes perfect sense.

Grants and matched funds

There are countless grants available from the UK government. Do some desk research and you'll find they come in many forms. Essentially, you'll need to prove that your business will provide jobs in the near future, and as you grow. Sometimes the grants come in the form of free consultancy from registered experts. It may not be cash, but it's as good as, if you were going to spend money on a specialist anyway.

It means you'll need to raise less cash, because of the 'free' consultants.

By matched funds, I mean situations where a government or related institution will say, for example, 'We will provide you with a non-returnable grant of £100,000 provided you match that with £100,000 from new investors.'

R&D tax credits

R&D tax credits work like this: if you hire a small team of software developers who you assign to the development of a new service or feature of your company's service offering, you can get real cash from the government to offset the costs of those development staff. You have to prove that they are R&D developers and not committed to ordinary day-to-day operations. You won't get the cash as soon as you employ the staff, but once the government acknowledges it owes you the funds you can often raise a bank loan or overdraft against that government commitment.

How much does crowdfunding cost?

What are the typical fees charged by the crowdfunding service companies?

As this is a dynamic market, it's best to make approaches to the companies of your choice and get them to quote. Their fees are pretty much in the public domain, so it will be easy to compare.

There are two main fees. First, the success fee for raising the funds. I've looked at Crowdcube, IndieGoGo and

Kickstarter, and the fees range from 4 per cent to 7 per cent. That means if you're raising £100,000 you would pay between £4,000 and £7,000, but only if the campaign is a success. There are usually no fees if your campaign fails to reach the target. Fees are VAT exempt.

Second, there are payment-processing fees, which can range from 0.5 per cent to a whopping 3 per cent–5 per cent. This is basically what a credit card processing company charges. Remember, many investments are very small – perhaps as small as £100 – so it's no surprise the card companies charge these fees. You will have to pay whether your campaign succeeds or not.

Overall you need to total up all the fees when making a comparison – I've noticed that the lowest success fees are associated with the highest card fees. What a surprise!

Should you want the platform to help you prepare your finances for the campaign, they will charge extra – upwards of £1,200, plus VAT.

How to judge if the fees are right and fair

Fees will almost certainly be divided into negotiable and non-negotiable. The points below indicate the factors that will help you determine how much you can haggle:

- Do they want you? If you're an exciting company in a hot sector, they'll bend. Why? Because you won't be helping their competition, and you'll add some 'showroom appeal' to encourage new investors and new companies seeking to raise funds.

- Are you raising large funds? If they're getting 6 per

cent core fees, then they can afford to waive set-up fees if there's enough money involved.

- There are easy line items they can give away. They might agree not to charge you a commission on investors that you secure as part of your pre-funding campaign with angels. After all, they come from your efforts, not theirs.

Case study: a successful crowdfunding campaign

The example I've taken is Sundried, which closed a round of £175,000 in August 2016.

I spoke to Daniel Puddick, MD, founder and largest shareholder in Sundried Ltd.

Sundried is a premium activewear brand with a focus on low-carbon and ethical production. Daniel started Sundried when he left his previous company in October 2015, and they had their first customer transaction in June 2016.

Sundried faced a common dilemma of needing funding but being spoilt for choice as to where to find it. They needed more capital to grow, but they knew they were too small for venture capital (VC) firms. Since they were a consumer brand, they liked the idea of reaching out to the large group of potential customers/investors that crowdfunding offers.

There was always the potential to go back to their original investors, but one of the investors in Daniel's first business wasn't in a position to invest again. Daniel could have underwritten a personal loan, but for various reasons, crowdfunding was the best bet at the time.

Before launching any crowdfunding campaign, you need to arrive at a pre-money valuation of the company, i.e. the value of the company before the new investment you're seeking. Sundried already had a small investment from the Low Carbon Innovation Fund, and that was at a pre-money valuation of £2m. Sundried felt that this valuation was too high for the new crowdfunding investors. Their crowdfunding company, Crowdcube, suggested a pre-money valuation of £1m, and they went with a compromise of £1.25m. They wisely knew that a VC firm would have really pushed them down on pre-money valuation. Another reason for crowdfunding; you're more in control of setting the valuation.

Rewards can often be an attractive 'sweetener' to an incoming investor and Sundried decided to offer rewards as part of the investor incentive. These formed part of the campaign, as they wanted all their potential investors to experience the products.

It's essential to have a clear reason for why you want to raise the money. Daniel was clear that it was to invest in their product range, to add people and to run their own triathlon event.

How much did they need? Daniel's financial model detailed that they would require investment of £400,000 over the next 1–2 years. However, he knew this would be a struggle for a crowdfunding campaign at their stage of development. His reading said that his own network would need to provide at least 50 per cent of any target. He was comfortable with £125,000 as a target, thinking that his own personal connections would get him close to the 50 per cent mark, or £62,500.

In the end, the campaign not only reached its target, it overshot. They raised £175,000, and so were over-funded by 40 per cent. They could have taken more, but Daniel was keen to get back to running the business full-time. Crowd-funding is distracting! They were offered the opportunity to extend the campaign but declined.

It's important after a campaign like this one to check where you stand in terms of your shareholder percentages of equity. Since Sundried had overshot, they actually issued shares so that the new investors ended up with 12.06 per cent of the company, instead of the originally planned 8.91 per cent. This 12.06 per cent was represented by 200 new investors.

Like many who will be reading this book, Daniel was cursorily aware of crowdfunding but had no prior experience of it before his campaign. He'd read the tech press and had followed how other companies had raised their funds. For Sundried, choosing a crowdfunding company was a project from scratch. In the end, they only looked at two companies. The one they didn't go with wanted retainer fees post-funding, which Sundried felt would have locked them in and restricted their ability to switch to another funder for subsequent rounds. They liked www.crowdcube.com, so they went with them.

Sundried didn't raise pre-pledges beforehand, apart from £10,000 that Daniel put in to start the campaign. Once it was underway, it was obvious they were going to have to rustle up investors themselves – 'big time', as Daniel put it – if they were going to set fire to the campaign.

Not far into the campaign, Crowdcube introduced them to an investor who, after a little negotiation, put in £40,000. Daniel's wife added a further £10,000 and then Daniel himself added a final £20,000, mid-campaign. His friends and contacts came in too. He thought they'd invest £10 or £100 here and there, but in practice, they put up larger numbers. All in all, they contributed around 50 per cent of the £125,000 target.

The Financial Conduct Authority (FCA) regulates the crowdfunding market to ensure it's fair and transparent. As such, they impose restrictions on the crowdfunding companies, one of which is that an individual investor can't make multiple investments in the same campaign. To do so would create the impression that the 'crowd' were behind the project and it was gathering investor acceptance. But, within reason, multiple investments are permissible, as was the case with Daniel and the Sundried campaign. Daniel said that had they dropped £40,000 at £1,000 a time, he was sure Crowdcube would have prevented it happening, but a single larger tranche was acceptable.

Due diligence is another obligation placed on crowdfunding companies by the FCA. This is the process by which all the claims made by the company are exhaustively verified. This can range from checking if one of the management team actually holds the position at the company they claim, all the way through to ensuring there is no litigation against the company.

In terms of pre-campaign tasks and materials, Daniel had already prepared a simple video, a financial model and a pitch deck, but was unprepared for the detail required for the due diligence. He noted that the detail required varied; on some occasions Sundried were asked for very extensive proof of something, while on another a photocopy of a business card sufficed as proof of Daniel's role at a prior company.

The campaign went pretty much according to plan, but for the scrabble to add momentum by getting investors themselves, but once they passed 50 per cent of target the rest seemed to fall into place.

And the six-million-dollar question: Did Daniel and Sundried feel well looked after by Crowdcube? Daniel felt the overall answer was 'yes'. He would have welcomed more of a 'heads-up' about the process and what to expect during the campaign, but his conclusion was that Crowdcube was very professional.*

Perhaps the most valuable insight Daniel was able to share with me was why he believed the campaign had been a success. He attributes the success to the fact that he had already founded and run a successful company before, that Sundried is an ethical company and that he is personally involved in the sports that their clothing ranges are used for. He believes this ensured there was a degree of trust and empathy created with their investors. That, and reaching the tipping point of 50 per cent of target early in the campaign.

Would they do anything differently if they ran the campaign again? Inevitably, Daniel was loath to change the formula that had worked, but did concede that he'd do much more work on lining-up investors next time.

I asked both Daniel and Crowdcube to pass on any general advice to anyone contemplating a crowdfunding campaign:

Daniel: 'Get organized well. Get your financial numbers completely sorted, do a marketing plan in advance, get

---

* Other excellent, large crowdfunding companies are available in the UK! There are also a number of smaller, specialized ones too. Don't always look to the largest or the best known to run your campaign for you.

a list in advance off your crowdfunding company of what must be proven during due diligence, and do all you can (in the video and in the copy on the crowd-funding pages) to reassure your investors you know what you're doing running your business! We would use it again at a later stage, as it's good for marketing and could easily sit alongside a VC round.'

Crowdcube offered some detailed advice:

Get investment ready

You'll need a detailed business plan and financial fore-casts readily available, so potential investors can evaluate your business and make a fully informed deci-sion about investing. The government offers attractive tax relief schemes of up to 50 per cent, such as the Enterprise Investment Scheme (EIS) and the Seed Enterprise Investment Scheme (SEIS), for small busi-ness investors. It's an important factor for crowd investors, so find out from the HMRC if your business is eligible.

Create a killer pitch

Start with a crystal-clear proposition that concisely out-lines what makes your business unique, the potential market opportunity and what the strategy for growth is. You're asking people to part with their money, so they have to believe in what they are investing in – not just the product, but also the people behind it. Make sure to highlight your credentials, history and expertise – and the team behind you.

Finally, outline the company's strategy for growth

and show that the business is scalable. Of course, any investor wants to know about the potential return on their investment, so it's critical that a business can outline how and when this could happen.

Engage your own crowd

Businesses that already have a network of existing customers and suppliers are at an advantage, so engage your existing community and offer them the opportunity to invest. Reaching the first 10 per cent of an investment target is the hardest part, so businesses that are able to leverage existing networks to raise investment and get early momentum are more likely to succeed.

Maintain the dialogue

You will get asked a lot of questions during your pitch and responding to those queries quickly goes a long way. Not only are they potential investors, but they are also potential customers, so treat the funding round as part of your customer experience – and that means not forgetting them after you fund, either. After all, your investors can become your biggest brand advocates or most valued business contact.

Reality check

This could be a six-month project – still want to go ahead?

If you've not just dipped into the book but are reading it sequentially, then you'll now know the different sources of funding and will be starting to get an idea of which might be best for your project. If you're too early for debt funding, then chances are you're heading for crowdfunding, and that requires a combination of angel funding to get a number of pre-pledges, followed by the crowdfunding campaign. As we move forward, that's going to be our focus.

Still much to do – but keep positive!

3:

HOW TO GET READY

Getting the basics organized

At this stage of your funding campaign, you have probably progressed this far:

— An idea for a business or a project, perhaps with some preliminary research from the internet about the market opportunities

— A registered company

— A bank account

— A domain name or URL

— Chosen one or more of the people who will form your management team

Don't be concerned if you're not even at this stage. Appendix I gives you guidance on how to set up a company and open a bank account.

It's definitely a good idea to think up a name for your business and see if the domain name is already taken. You can do that easily via many domain name registrars. (I tend to use easyhost.com.)

There's much more detail on choosing a domain name in Appendix II, but it's worth flagging here that the jury's out as to whether to go for '.com'. My general advice is go for a domain that is memorable, even if it means you only get the '.co.uk' domain and the main derivatives such as '.eu'. So, if you register www.mybigidea.co.uk even though www. mybigidea.com is already taken, it is wise to get all the main domains you can, such as www.mybigidea.eu or www. mybigidea.biz. Your competition may be able to spend more than you on Google AdWords, and their domain will be the first people see on a Google search if you give them the chance.

Now it's time for some fundamental questions. What's your big idea? Is there a real need for it? How will your idea fulfil that need? Is it unique, and can it sustain that status? Is it scalable? Financially sound? Do you have a credible go-to-market plan? What competition could stop it succeeding? Do you have the right team?

If there's a crunch section of this book, then this is it. However disciplined you are at planning and implementing a crowdfunding campaign, you're only as good as the business idea you put to investors.

Here's my simple list of what you need to consider. The list is for those who are starting a business, but could equally apply if you are raising funds for, say, a charitable cause.

— What's the problem?
— How big is the problem?
— How can it be fixed?
— What's your plan to do that?
— Will it make money?
— How will you make the most money possible?
— What might stop you?

— What's your evidence? = traction

— Why you're the people to do it

— Make me a deal

What's the problem?

Pretty much every investor nowadays wants to start with knowing the problem you're trying to solve, often referred to as the 'market pain'.

Some (not original) examples might be:

— Why don't London taxis offer fixed-price journeys?

— Art gallery audio guides are so 'last century', can't they be interactive?

— Why can't I pay for petrol at a filling station from an app?

— Why isn't there a single website that sources groceries at best price from many shops?

— I can't find a single app or website that will find me the best car lease deal

— I want to have dinner in Oxford next week – can I get restaurants to bid for my custom?

— Why can't train companies use social media to tell me where there are empty seats on my train?

— I wish there was a device in all my things that linked to my phone so I never lost them

The message is this: there has to be a need for what you want to do. It all boils down to saving time, saving money, making you money, being able to do something easily that was hard to do before, having fun or making you safer.

How big is the problem?

This is all about the size of your market now, and the size of your plan. Don't confuse market with industry. Fast food is an industry, but setting up a fast food restaurant in, say, Brighton, is entering the market for fast food in Brighton. It's a common mistake, even among business school alumni, to quote values of industries as if the bigger the number, the more credible their plan becomes. But if there's no market where you're positioning your business, then the size of the industry doesn't matter. It matters, of course, if the industry is small and you are claiming a massive revenue over the years ahead. Watch repair is a £125m a year industry in the UK, so if anyone tried to get me to invest in a watch-repair business that forecasted a revenue of £75m in year five, I wouldn't believe it, and it would make me sceptical as to how grounded and realistic this team was.

What matters here is the 'addressable market'. If your business was running a restaurant providing 'fusion' food in Brighton – maybe a combination of Asian and Latin American cuisine – your addressable market would, in theory, be the sum value of the turnover of all Asian and Latin American restaurants in the area. But in reality, if you were the first fusion restaurant, your addressable market would be the percentage of that sum value that would be prepared to switch, at a certain frequency, to go to your restaurant or your competition's as well. Often, an honest look at addressable markets results in your business's potential being quite small, and that may cause you to re-think exactly what you are proposing to do. On the other hand, there are obvious growth industries within which sub-markets will flourish. Lithium battery and other energy businesses, retirement homes, long-term health businesses and ethical manufacturing come to mind.

How can it be fixed?

'How can the problem be fixed?' is not the same as asking 'what's your plan?' A solution to a problem may not have a viable plan. Solving the problem of overcrowding on trains by developing an app that dynamically allocates travel times to flexi-hour commuters sounds very clever. But you then need to check if your solution is feasible. And it being feasible means someone, somewhere will pay for it, and they'll do so sustainably, i.e. continuously and at an adequate gross margin (more of which later).

One of the approaches to this at London Business School is to switch away from business plans and towards feasibility plans. In his excellent book *The New Business Road Test*, Professor John Mullins devised a methodology for testing seven critical factors, which, if effectively addressed, combine to make a business likely to be successful. His thinking is that entrepreneurs rarely have one idea, and his book addresses the question, 'Which of my ideas should I devote time to at the next stage of development?' Put simply, you should work on the idea that has the best chance of winning in its market.

What's your plan to do that?

If you're raising early-stage capital – in the £150,000 to £300,000 range – then you're going to need practical details on how your business will work. This means the price the customer will pay, the cost of selling and delivering the product or service to the customer, the plan for doing that selling (such as advertising, or a direct or agency sales force), the resources needed to produce the product (whether that's an editorial team, or cooks in a trade kitchen who are making your produce), your staff costs and your other overheads (the regular and recurring costs of capital equipment you'll have to purchase). These are just the financial numbers. You will also need to explain *how* you'll do it. For example, say you're going to make furniture for cafes in London. Your plan might be to design the furniture and give away much of your margin to a woodworking or fabrication company for the first year, but then bring manufacturing in-house when your turnover can support dedicated premises.

Will it make money?

Making money, of course, is about making profit. But there is a quality facet to profits, and the secret is nearly always in the gross margin.

How will you make the most money possible?

This is all about being a market leader. There's a rule of thumb that in e-commerce, as well as in most other markets,

60 per cent of the market is usually shared by the three market leaders, and 80 per cent is shared between the top five.

In practical terms, you're going to need to imagine holding around 25 per cent–30 per cent of your chosen market if you are going to be a market leader. The significant thing to consider here is to what degree the market for your service or product can co-exist with the competition.

For example, back in 2003 there were two business social networks that carried your CV and enabled you to make contact with other business people. There were Xing (www.xing.com) founded 1 November 2003 in Hamburg, Germany, and LinkedIn (www.linkedin.com), founded in California and launched on 5 May 2003. The market only really needed one such company, and Xing was the loser internationally. It is still a very successful business, and retains a near €1bn (£850m) market cap through its dominance in the German market. LinkedIn, however, was bought by Microsoft in January 2017 for $26.2bn (£21bn).

There is nearly always some sort of competition in what you do. It can be direct competition, like a clothing store near to others catering for a similar demographic of consumer, or it can be a substitute, the way video conferencing is a substitute for travel and hotel accommodation.

You must think through not just who or what the competition might be, but what you have to do in order to get the market share to be in the top three – and if there is room for more than one service like yours out there.

It must be said that it's very expensive to go for the 'winner takes all' position in a market where the consumer only needs one of the services. Uber, the app-based private-hire taxi service, has raised a total of $10bn but continues to seek funds – such is the very high cost of making totally sure it stays the dominant provider.

Paradoxically, competition is usually good – it validates a sector. In the car industry, for example, cars that fall outside a clearly identifiable segment – compact SUVs, say – often struggle for market share and sales. One example is the underselling Fiat 500X, a fantastic car which missed getting onto buyers' shortlists because it has no obvious direct competition.

What might stop you?

Clearly competition can stop you, but what else? This book deals more with getting 'investment-ready' rather than giving operational advice. But investors will ask hypothetical questions and you need to imagine how you might deal with them if they occur. I know it sounds negative, but make a list of all the things that could go wrong. Here's a start:

Shareholders

A change of control, a ratchet or warrant exercised, a new 'difficult' director being imposed on you, or a change in the shareholders' agreement giving shareholders more control over day-to-day activities.

Cash

You don't raise enough and compromise your plan, perhaps with too little marketing money, or you get your forecast wrong and need more staff to do the job, or you simply get your budget wrong, underperform and need more cash from your shareholders.

Sales

Your product or service suffers from a weak proposition and sales fall or fail to meet targets, or strong competition forces you to drop your prices, your sales team prove to be inadequate and it takes time to replace them, or you don't get your marketing right in support of sales, or your systems to support sales (like CRM – Customer Relationship Management – software) underperform.

Margins

Your suppliers have the upper hand, or your customers beat the price down, or you have to borrow money and the cost of that money reduces your margins and profitability, or the currency conversion costs for your international customers rise and the pound sterling goes against you. Or, simply, your operating costs are higher than expected.

People

They underperform, they cost more than you thought, they resign and leave you in the lurch, or they work well at their job but damage the culture of your company with their attitude.

Trading performance

You fail to track with KPI charts (Key Performance Indicators), or fail to set realistic targets.

Business continuity

This could be a systems failure, a fire, a break-in, a power-cut, hacking, or simply an ex-employee with a grudge.

Brand and core proposition

You lose sight of who you are as a company, your reason for existing, your goals and how the market and your customers see you.

Litigation

A customer, a supplier, a member of staff, or another entity decides to take legal action against you and you lose valuable time, money and reputation as a result.

What's your evidence? = traction

Investors want to know if you have any evidence that your idea will work. It reduces the risk of failure – and therefore their loss of investment funds – if you can name some trends of market acceptance, commonly known as traction.

Traction is usually focused on sales. If your dress designs are already accepted by a major retailer, even to the extent of a pilot order, or your FinTech software idea is focus-group tested but you've yet to start volume sales, then you probably have the beginnings of traction.

If you've already used the money from a former 'Friends & Family' fundraise to secure those early metrics (objective measurable data) then, to be investment ready, you're going to have to show they can be projected forwards with credibility.

Sometimes projection is easy. Say, for example, you've run a Google AdWords campaign with limited funds – perhaps £25,000. What it may have shown is that you can acquire page views to your website at £40 per 1000 visitors. If you've been tracking what happens to those visitors and you know that, say, one in every hundred buy your product or service, then you have a metric. Let's say it suggests that you need to pay £40 to sell ten units of your service or product (1/100 × 1000). So, each unit sold has cost you £4 in marketing costs. If the margin of that product is 25 per cent, (meaning the balance of 75% is the cost of making it) and you sell for £20 each, then your gross margin is £5 (25 per cent of £20). This means your net margin (gross margin less cost of sales) is £1. As you scale the business, the financial plan you present to investors might indicate that you expect to improve your gross margin from 25 per cent to 35 per cent, and that your efficiency in buying AdWords will increase so that the cost per 1000 views comes down to £30. And let's imagine also that your website gets slicker at converting those leads, so that instead of 1/100 conversions, you achieve 5/100.

Then the economics look more like this: The cost of sales per unit is now £0.60 (5 sales at a marketing cost of £30). The gross margin is now £7 (35 per cent of £20). The metrics are starting to look great, with a net margin of £6.40 (£7 less £0.6).

Provided in this example, you can show market evidence that other companies have achieved those improvements, your current traction can be extrapolated in the improved figures we've shown.

However, it's in the nature of investors to be conservative. When preparing your financial plan, build a tolerance into your numbers – use, for example, 75 per cent of everything you measure. But never, ever, use the words 'this model is very conservative'! Every investor has heard that a hundred times or more. We investors like to know, in real numbers, what you think you can achieve and to see the risk effect, mostly in terms of cash burn, of what happens if you underperform.

Not all traction is to do with marketing and sales. It could be that to run a profitable pizza home-delivery company you need to have a securely contracted source of raw food materials. A measure of traction in this case will be a contract for the supply of flour, for example. Your business might be in Scotland and your customers predominantly in the South East. What evidence do you have that you can secure transportation within the figures you've put in your plan?

Traction is mostly about customer acceptance of your idea or your product. Focus groups help. Perhaps a tasting session for a wine you've been importing in small quantities, but now want to upscale?

The more you can show traction, the more likely you are to build trust and acceptance from a prospective investor. And that, in turn, will be reflected in the pre-money valuations you'll be able to attach to your company.

Why you're the people to do it

There's a cliché in the world of investing that the three factors which matter when deciding to invest in a business are management, management and management.

It's certainly true that a great management team can turn a lacklustre idea into a commercial success, just as surely as a weak team can fail to deliver on a commercially sound business plan.

As you'll have seen above, I subscribe to the idea that investors start with the idea, the problem it's solving, its viability, defensibility, scalability and lastly, its deliverability by the team.

As such, there is evidence from the crowdfunding community that your probability of hitting your crowdfunding target is increased by the number of people you have in the team:

If you have four or more people on your team, you'll raise 70 per cent more money than if you only have one person.[4]

Here are some other factors relating to your team which will impress investors (but don't worry if you can't 'tick off' the whole list):

- You've built a company already and sold it with a valuable exit valuation.

- The team shows strong know-how in the sector your company is in.

- The team is balanced, with a good spread of skills – general management, marketing, sales, tech skills, etc.

- You've worked in larger companies before – this means you'll have budgeting and other professional disciplines covered.

- You already have good, long-standing relations with professional advisers: accountants, lawyers, PR companies, ad agencies, HR recruitment firms, website or other software developers, etc.

- Good team chemistry – cohesive, supportive, mutually respectful, non-competitive within the team, plus personal characteristics like humour and approachability.

- Evidence that the whole team is committed to the project. A good sign is that you are *all* working full-time on the business you're seeking funding for. Less good is that only one of you is working full-time, with the rest of the team in other full-time employment until funding is secured.

- Commitment to personal investment. 'Sweat equity', meaning shares in return for working on the project ahead of funding, is less credible than real cash committed to the business. The sum doesn't need to be massive, just enough to have what investors call 'skin in the game', meaning you're sharing the risk and the investor can rest assured that you'll try your hardest to make the business a success.

- Lastly, I place integrity high in the core values of a team. You don't have to be dishonest to succeed in business; honesty, openness and transparency of information – good and bad – will build trust. But one lie or bending of the truth will totally undermine the trust you'll have worked hard to build with your potential investors. They will think, 'If they weren't straight about that data, what else might they be hiding?'

4:

HOW TO MAKE A FINANCIAL PLAN

At the core of any business plan is the financial model. And there's no investor that will be unfamiliar with a spreadsheet.

Your task is to lay out a spreadsheet – using Microsoft's Excel or Apple's Numbers – that achieves the following:

- Gives a clear picture of how the business will grow over the next three or five years in terms of revenue and profits.

- Shows how much cash the company will need to reach profitability – and illustrates how the cash requirement might vary if the company under- or overperforms.

- Provides calculations which illustrate the return on investment your investor will get.

- Shows the cap table. This is a separate table that details the capital history. It lists all the shareholders, the shares they own and what price they paid for their shares. It's important for potential investors, because it tells the story of how the value of your company has grown since your very first 'round' of investment (see chapter 6 for more on this).

To achieve all this, your spreadsheet will need to:

- Show past trading performance linked seamlessly to your forecast of how the business will perform after the funding.

- Give a clear picture of how the revenue will be generated.

- Show cost of sales (like commissions or direct costs associated with each sale).

- Detail the staff costs – the salaries or consulting fees that will be paid, when the staff member will join you, and what additional costs they will incur, like national insurance, recruitment, etc.

- Provide a detailed list of all other operating costs – from office premises, to marketing, to tech resources.

- Make assumptions regarding the P/E (price–earnings ratio – or the multiple of year 3 or year 5 earnings that will form one measure of valuation at the end of the time you'll take to build the business).

- Make assumptions about a 'discount rate' – the per cent figure that the business model spreadsheet will use to bring the long-term value of the business back into 'today's money' at a future date.[5]

Usually, investors like to see P&L (Profit and Loss) details for the first three years, then quarterly summaries for year 4 onwards. But more than anything, they like to see how much cash the business will need and when it will become

CUMULATIVE CASH FLOW					
JAN-17	FEB-17	MAR-17	APR-17	MAY-17	JUN-17
(1,250)	(9,535)	(44,742)	(78,341)	(113,902)	(142,866)
JUL-17	AUG-17	SEP-17	OCT-17	NOV-17	DEC-17
(144,303)	(144,682)	(148,960)	(149,761)	(149,367)	(125,345)
JAN-18	FEB-18	MAR-18	APR-18	MAY-18	JUN-18
(161,337)	(151,043)	(178,052)	(145,715)	(160,166)	(126,159
		BREAK-EVEN			
JUL-18	AUG-18	SEP-18	OCT-18	NOV-18	DEC-18
(86,677)	(76,451)	(42,971)	13,434	32,939	84,322
JAN-19	FEB-19	MAR-19	APR-19	MAY-19	JUN-19
144,688	165,894	219,605	297,997	343,668	430,028
JUL-19	AUG-19	SEP-19	OCT-19	NOV-19	DEC-19
534,486	603,200	702,435	823,006	908,612	1,027,066

cash positive – that's when the cash coming in from customers exceeds the costs of running the business.

In our example – Cumulative Cash Flow (see figure above) — I've illustrated how to show the maximum cash required. I've indicated that the business will go into profit/cash in the March of year 2. Or, in other words, at the end of the fifteenth month.

We now know it's at cash break-even, because your plan shows the maximum amount of cash required is £178,052, whereas in month 16 (April 2018), that figure drops to £145,715, meaning the company has made £32,337 (that's £178,052 max, plus £32,337 positive cash, leaving £145,715).

If this was your business and I was your potential investor, I would be thinking, 'OK, this business needs at least £178,052. If they hit all their targets that would mean that if

I gave them the £178,052 they would use that up over the fifteen months and there would be exactly zero in the bank account. That's too risky; they may miss their targets and I don't want them to run out of cash. I'm going to suggest they ask for, perhaps, £200,000, to give themselves some headroom.'

There is always a difference between the P&L figures and the cash-flow figures. The easiest way to explain this is to think of a company in which a product is sold in, say, January, but payment from the customer is not received for thirty days. The profit in January is the value of the service or goods sold to the customer, but the cash is zero. In February, the profit might be the same as January but the cash figure will reflect the money received from the customer who bought your service in January, and has now paid. As you build your model, adding, hopefully, ever growing rates of sales, you'll build a complete picture of your profits and all the delayed, or staggered, receipts of cash. This is important, as it's your cash flow that will determine how much funding you need.

Don't be put off by the preparation of the financial picture of the business. There will be lots of help out there to prepare your financial model. What's important is that you understand the model, and are word perfect (or number perfect) on the figures.

You must get yourself in a position to be able to answer these basic questions an investor might ask:

- What will the revenue for this business be in each of the first five years of your trading?

- What losses and then profits will you make over that period?

- How will your gross margin develop? This is your revenue less your cost of sales expressed as a percentage. It's a measure of risk – low gross margin businesses like retail or white goods are vulnerable to price-cutting by competition.

- What's the mix of your operating costs over the period? You should be able to build a photographic memory of this if you create a pie chart of your operating costs for each of your forecast years. That way, it's easy to visualize that, for example, your expenditure on marketing will fall as a per cent of all costs from 35 per cent in year 1 to 25 per cent in year 5. Why? Well, it might be because other costs have risen – such as building a bigger team, or it could simply be that as your brand gets better known you will be able to reduce your cost of acquisition for each customer.

- What's your cost of acquisition in relation to the lifetime value of your customer? This is the cost of your marketing, or the direct sales force costs for each customer or order. The lifetime value might be the average time a customer stays with you multiplied by the subscription rate of your service – say 14 months X £10 p/m = £140. The cost of acquiring the customer might be £37. So, the 'payback' on spending to get the customer may be recovered in 3.8 months (140/37), or expressed as a percentage, in this case 26 per cent (37/140).

- How much cash are you raising, and what margin are you giving yourself over the maximum negative cash shown in the model? The model may show your bank account running dry after you've spent, say, £180,000, before the monthly profits start to kick in. The margin here refers to the extra allowance you are making for things not going according to plan. You will need to make some 'what if' calculations to see what effect they have on your cash flow and your maximum negative cash position. You might plug into your model sales being down by 25 per cent and operating costs up by 15 per cent, and see what that does. Some models are very sensitive. But if, in the worst 'what if' you could imagine, the cash required jumped to, say, £230,000, I would suggest you add a 25 per cent margin on the top of that. This would be £287,500, rounded to, say, £290,000. The more breathing room the better.

- What actions will you take to reduce costs should you underperform, so as not to run out of cash? Run the model again to test these assumptions.

- What is my investment return expressed in terms of a multiple and as an IRR per cent (Internal Rate of Return per cent)? Multiple simply means money in vs money out. Say the investor puts £50,000 into your business and takes 4.8 per cent of the equity. If the business is worth £5,000,000 in five years' time, then the investor will own 4.8 per cent of that, which is £238,095. Their money in was £50,000 and their money out is £238,095, so the multiple return is 4.76. In terms of IRR per cent, this equates to an annual rate of return, as if the money was earning interest. In our example, this works out at

36.6 per cent per annum. See figure below for the numbers.

	YEAR 1	YEAR 2	YEAR 3	YEAR 4	YEAR 5
VALUE OF COMPANY BEFORE INVESTMENT	1,000,000				
INVESTOR MONEY	50,000				
VALUE AFTER INVESTMENT	1,050,000				
LONG-TERM VALUE OF THE COMPANY					5,000,000
RATE OF RETURN REQUIRED	37%	37%	37%	37%	37%
VALUE OF THE COMPANY AFTER EACH YEAR	1,050,000	1,434,648	1,960,205	2,678,291	3,659,434	5,000,000
INVESTOR SHARE	4.8%	4.8%	4.8%	4.8%	4.8%	4.8%
VALUE OF INVESTOR'S MONEY	50,000	68,317	93,343	127,538	174,259	238,095
	MONEY IN: 50,000		MONEY OUT: 238,095		MULTIPLE: 4.76	

Justifying the money you want

In this chapter we've covered how to assess the amount of money you should raise, depending upon the maximum negative cash of your business plan adjusted for the risk of you not hitting your sales targets or operating cost budget.

But you'll still need to justify why you need the money, and explain what you'll do with it. The expression used in investor circles is 'use of funds'.

This is really all about showing that the money is predominantly going where the investors want it to go, which is towards building the business. Money spent on creating revenue and reducing churn or cancellations should feature largely – that's marketing or advertising spend, direct sales staff and customer support.

Investors don't want to see high fixed salaries going to the executive team, or to a chairperson or non-executive directors. Do your best to make senior salaries progressive – i.e. low until the business is breaking even in cash-flow terms – and ideally linked to success. Your package and that of your senior team members might be linked to the company's performance by as much as 50 per cent of the package. Ideally, the non-execs, if you need them, shouldn't take any cash out of the business, but in any event they should either waive their fees in year 1, or have their fees convertible into equity.

There's no magic number to try and conform to, as all businesses are different. But as a general rule, highlight the spend on factors that will drive the business model, and illustrate what actions you've taken to keep costs down. These might include working out of an incubator to save office rental costs, using a sales agency to make cold calls by paying them commission only, or doing a deal with your software developer where they share in revenue up to, say, 125 per cent of what they would have invoiced you for.

As with almost everything to do with raising funds, your objective is to get the investor to trust you. By showing that you're treating their potential investment with care, you are aligning yourself with their thinking and demonstrating that you'll be watching their cash and costs for the lifetime of the company.

How much of the company (in shares) should I be giving away?

This is as big a question as any entrepreneur asks themselves.

Here's all the maths you need:

	EXAMPLE 1	EXAMPLE 2
PRE-MONEY VALUATION	750,000	500,000
NEW INVESTORS' CASH	250,000	250,000
POST MONEY VALUATION	1,000,000	750,000
NEW INVESTORS' EQUITY		
CASH IN	250,000	250,000
POST MONEY VALUATION	1,000,000	750,000
% CASH IN REPRESENTS	25%	33%

In Example 1, you could set the pre-money valuation at £750,000. That is the current value you assign to your business. You can see that this means the investors get 25 per cent of the equity 'cake' after the funding round has closed. But if that pre-money drops to £500,000, then the investor gets 33 per cent.

Investors usually haggle around the percentage of equity they'll get for their investment. The pre-money valuation is really only a mechanism to 'tune' the percentage of the company's shares your investors are going to get.

The pre-money valuation is also a function of the intended investment return. So, by extending our example table above, adding the expected valuation in the future when you exit (sell) your company, you get the following calculations:

	EXAMPLE 1	EXAMPLE 2
PRE-MONEY VALUATION	750,000	500,000
NEW INVESTORS' CASH	250,000	250,000
POST MONEY VALUATION	1,000,000	750,000
NEW INVESTORS' EQUITY		
CASH IN	250,000	250,000
POST MONEY VALUATION	1,000,000	750,000
% CASH IN REPRESENTS	25%	33%
VALUATION AT EXIT	5,000,000	5,000,000
INVESTOR SHARE ON EXIT	1,250,000	1,666,667
NEW INVESTOR CASH IN	250,000	250,000
MULTIPLE OF CASH IN TO CASH OUT	5.0	6.7
IMPROVEMENT (EXAMPLE 1 IS THE BASE CASE SO 0%)	0%	33%

This shows that by haggling the valuation down, the investor now has a chance of making 6.7 times his or her money, as opposed to 5 times their money with the higher valuation. That's a 33 per cent improvement.

If you can't agree on the valuation, don't let this lose you the investor. If you're running an angel investor campaign then you can change the valuation right up to the last moment. Likewise with a crowdfunding campaign. But a better bet is to keep the valuation fixed and offer to adjust the valuation with the issuance of shares if you fail to hit performance targets.

Let's say that you and your investor group can't agree on the pre-money valuation. They want £500,000 and you want £750,000. The solution is to stick with your valuation of £750,000, but offer the investors additional shares free of charge in the event you don't hit your commercial targets. You could say that you have a target of £300,000 of sales in your first year and if you hit that then you don't issue them any more shares.

But you might say that if you only achieve £200,000 of sales you will 'gift' them whatever number of shares it takes for the implicit valuation to be £500,000 – the figure they wanted.

You can have a sliding scale between the two. It would look like this:

	EXAMPLE 1	EXAMPLE 2
PRE-MONEY VALUATION	750,000	500,000
NEW INVESTORS' CASH	250,000	250,000
POST MONEY VALUATION	1,000,000	750,000
NEW INVESTORS' EQUITY		
CASH IN	250,000	250,000
POST MONEY VALUATION	1,000,000	750,000
% CASH IN REPRESENTS	25%	33%
VALUATION AT EXIT	5,000,000	5,000,000
INVESTOR SHARE ON EXIT	1,250,000	1,666,667
NEW INVESTOR CASH IN	250,000	250,000
MULTIPLE OF CASH IN TO CASH OUT	5	7
IMPROVEMENT (EXAMPLE 1 IS THE BASE CASE SO 0%)	0%	33%
NUMBER OF SHARES (AT PRE-MONEY STAGE)	750,000	750,000
PRICE PER SHARE £	1.00	0.67
SHARES ISSUED FOR A £250,000 INVESTMENT	250,000	375,000
ADDITIONAL SHARES TO BE ISSUED	375,000	EX 2
	250,000	LESS EX 1
	125,000	BALANCE

To compensate investors who wanted a £500,000 pre-money valuation but initially agreed to go along with your

£750,000 valuation, you'd have to issue them with 125,000 more shares to bring them up to a shareholding they would have got had the valuation been £500,000 from the outset.

The sliding scale means that if you achieved sales of £200,000 instead of £300,000, the investors would get the full 125,000 additional shares. But if, for example, you achieved £250,000 of sales, then, since this is halfway between £200,000 and £300,000, you would issue them with additional shares half way along the scale, which would be 50 per cent of 125,000 additional shares, which is 62,500 shares. The implicit valuation would then be £625,000 (£750,000 less £500,000 = £250,000. Divide by 2 = £125,000. So, £125,000 more than £500,000 is £625,000).

This may all seem complicated, but in practice it's very simple. The advantage is that everyone is OK with the deal, and you've solved the issue of agreeing the valuation before the funding.

One word of caution. This might negate the opportunity to allow your investors to claim SEIS or EIS tax relief – see Appendix IV.

I'm afraid you won't get much help from the crowdfunding companies on where to pitch your initial valuation. Their reluctance is simply because they don't want to accept any responsibility for the estimate: if the campaign fails they don't want to be blamed for making the shares too expensive. Look out for the spurious claim that it's a regulatory condition imposed by the Financial Conduct Authority. It's not!

Carlos Eduardo Espinal has written an excellent article on valuing start-ups. In summary, he suggests that the biggest determiners of your start-up's value are the market forces of the industry and sector in which it plays, which include the balance (or imbalance) between demand and supply of money, the recency and size of recent exits, the willingness for an investor to pay a premium to get into a deal, and the level of desperation of the entrepreneur looking for money.[6]

Final thoughts on how much to ask for

This really is a sense check at this stage of your planning. Hopefully you've already done the big work on your model, its cash flow, and therefore your funding need.

Remember to add the crowdfunding fees into your fundraise total. Paying a designer to tidy up your Word docs and your PowerPoint might cost a few hundred pounds, as might professional-quality pictures of you and the team. Then you should allow up to £2,000 for the video production, a further £500 for an event to kick-off the campaign, perhaps the same for another event mid-campaign and lastly, you will have the fees owed to the crowdfunding company. They will be around 6 per cent – so you'll need an additional £12,000 for a £200,000 raise. And remember to budget for legal fees – probably around £1,500.

The really big question here is, where does the money get you? Are you raising just enough to prove your business idea has traction? Or is it to get to break-even? Both are fine. You just need to be clear. Investors need to buy into a credible plan on the money side. Your justification might go like this:

> To take a 25 per cent share of our addressable market (which itself is growing at 15 per cent per annum) we'll need to be turning over around £5m at the end of year

3 of our plan. We'll need a retained customer base of 2,500 users by then, each contributing around £200 per month in revenue. Our funding requirement of £250,000 will permit us to prove we can attract each customer at a cost of £100 over the first 18 months. With this proof of traction, we will seek a further £250,000 to carry us past our month 24 break-even point and leave surplus funds to tactically enhance our product range or outpace our competitors with an accelerated customer acquisition programme as required.

Tip: The best advice I ever had was from the highly successful visionary, entrepreneur and venture capitalist Hermann Hauser, who told me, 'Always ask for more than you need, and always take more if it's offered even if you haven't asked.'

5:

HOW TO TELL YOUR STORY

This chapter will help you clarify the way you gather and present everything about your business.

Preparing a compelling description of your idea and why it will work

The key questions here are, 'What problem am I solving?' and 'How valuable is my solution?'

I often joked during the dot-com boom of the late nineties that pretty much any idea could get funded. My frivolous idea was www.adultery.com. This was a website on which you could deliver clean underwear, toothbrush and other essentials at any time during the night within London's orbital ring road, the M25. Clearly a need/problem, but probably not a big market (I hope!).

Whatever the idea, you have to communicate it as compellingly and succinctly as you can. Why? Because during the funding campaign you will tell your story over a pint in a pub, round a dinner table with friends, sitting next to someone on a bus or train or plane, standing next to someone in a queue, during a chance meeting at a conference in a cafe, or even in a lift – which is, of course, where the expression 'Elevator Pitch' comes from.

And that's just verbal communication. You'll need to

drop the essence of what you are funding into an email, into a tweet, into a LinkedIn post and into other written media. So here's a good example:

> We're raising £360,000 of equity funds for LawyerFair, offering 20 per cent of the equity in return. We help SMEs solve their legal problems, which they submit via our online platform to our vetted nationwide panel of over 35 law firms. These then bid competitively for the work, with a fixed price. With over 1,200 bids processed, our customers welcome the transparency and control of the costs, get very rapid responses, and, as a result, always deal with law firms who are experts for that particular task. What's more, in its January 2016 industry review, the Law Society specifically identified services such as ours as pointing the way to how legal services will be procured in the future.

The objective is NOT to encourage someone to pull out his or her chequebook, but to arouse their interest. It's all about starting a dialogue. The follow-up might be to arrange to meet, or to send them some supporting documents, but the primary objective is to get their contact details, so you can start that dialogue.

Telling your story – preparing an executive summary, short video, and a PowerPoint presentation

My suggestion is that you do the financial model first, then tell the whole story in the PowerPoint (or other presentation software), then prepare the executive summary, then script the video.

In the past, I've used a live-streamed TV programme from a studio to good effect. See chapter 7 for how to organize this and use it once your campaign has already started.

Three quick headlines for you on visual media:

- An executive summary is a two-pager that ideally looks professionally laid out and gives a snapshot of your business and the investment proposition. Its purpose is to engage an investor and lead to a meeting or a request for more information.

- Nowadays, you cannot get away without a video for a crowdfunding campaign. It's the effortless way to grab attention and lock a viewer into an uninterrupted three minutes of their time.

- You will need software: Microsoft's PowerPoint, Apple's Keynote, or Prize's Prezi. This is the way that top consulting firms now present strategic plans to clients. It's the best way to engage your potential investor, because it allows you to carry your investor on a journey from knowing nothing about you and not caring particularly, to understanding and interest. It's also the best format to allow your investor to pass your information to a fellow investor. It has to tell your story in a way that is easily understood, even if you're not telling it in person.

The executive summary

Your executive summary needs to cover the key aspects of any investor proposition:

- How much is being raised and how much equity is being given in return

- What's the problem and how big is the opportunity

- What's our solution and how we're going to make money

- Why now is a good time to raise the money and start the project and what we will do with the money

- Credibility – what traction has been achieved so far and what evidence there is that the customers like our solution

- Why our approach is unique and why we will beat the competition

- A small table showing a summary of the financial projections

- A little information on the management team

- How to get in touch

Not much more needs to be said about the content, other than try to make the copy light and interesting. I always think short sentences are more compelling to read. After all, that's how we communicate verbally – and you are 'speaking' to the one person who's reading it. This document will be used either as a follow-up to the approach email or at the same time, as an attachment to the email. The executive summary's objective is to foster engagement and lead to a request for more data, a phone call or a meeting.

The short video

Here are six tips for getting it right:

1. Video and audio quality are important. Shooting high-quality video on an iPhone or Android device is possible, but make sure the phone is on a tripod (or other stabilizing device) and the audio is clear. For lighting, record your video in a well-lit room or outside to get the optimal results. Before you hit action, shoot a sample scene. Look at it on your computer to make sure the lighting is correct and clear.

Consider buying a clip-on microphone that plugs into your phone rather than using the built-in audio, which will sound hollow the further you get from your phone. Speak loudly, clearly, and have the phone at an appropriate distance to get good quality. Listen to a sample, and if it sounds too hollow or if every time you say a word that starts with a 'p' the sound pops, do it again. Trial and error is the key here.

2. Don't try to wing it. Unless you are a trained public speaker, don't ad lib your video. Write a script and make sure it hits all the key points of your crowdfunding campaign. Like a journalist writing a news story, include the who, what, when, where and why of your campaign. Read it out loud and revise it until it is perfect. Then practise. You should sound natural when you shoot the final product.

3. Mention only two or three rewards. Going through an entire list of rewards is one of the most common mistakes I see in crowdfunding videos. People don't want to hear you drone on about every reward being offered. Instead, highlight only two or three of your best rewards. You want to get the viewer excited about what you are giving away through some of your best rewards, because enthusiasm is contagious and drives donations. For the remaining rewards, just include a simple reminder telling the viewer that the entire list is on your project page.

4. Keep it short and end with a bang! When making any video, follow the KISS rule: Keep It Simple, Stupid. You're not Martin Scorsese; nobody wants to sit through three hours of your filming, especially when you are asking them to fork out cash for your project.

The video should be short, exciting and get the viewer fired up to read more about what you are offering. Ideally, the video should be three minutes long or less (although really great videos will hold the audience's attention even if they're a little longer). For those who tend to ramble, keep in mind that with a crowdfunding campaign you have an entire page online to write out more details and to show photos that supplement the video. People have busy lives and short attention spans. Don't lose your viewers before getting to the most important part – asking for donations and help spreading the word about your campaign.

5. Don't forget 'the ask'. Every successful salesperson in the world will tell you that if you do not ask for a sale, you will not get it. In your video, be sure to ask for a donation and for help spreading the crowdfunding project to the viewer's friends and social-media network. 'The ask' should be clear, carefully worded and create a sense of urgency and action. Tell people specifically what to do: don't leave it up to them to figure it out on their own. But make sure it is sincere, as this authentic message can turn a viewer into a donor and marketing machine.

6. Turn to others. Look at other successful crowdfunding campaigns and watch their videos for inspiration. People who have successfully raised a lot of money through crowdfunding typically have very good videos. Learn from their experience.

The PowerPoint

There are many 'schools of thought' regarding the preparation of your PowerPoint 'deck', or 'slides', as they used to be called.

I favour the preparation of one complete set, from which I create two versions; one for sending, the other for presenting. The difference is that the one for sending can be more complex and hold more data. The one you present needs to be very simple, with extensive use of images that you talk around rather than 'pages' full of complex text.

The easiest way to prepare a presentation deck is to create it in Microsoft Word first and then cut and paste into the PowerPoint pages. By doing this, you won't get bogged down with formatting, colours and graphics; you can concentrate on telling the story.

A good rule of thumb is to state a fact and then explain what that means for your business and your investor. You always need to convert everything you say into a benefit. Some examples for the presenting version:

> 'The table below illustrates our compound growth rate in years 1, 2 and 3. This growth means we hit our break-even target in month 26.'

> 'Our Commercial Director, John Smith, has worked in the biochemistry industry for twenty years. His experience will ensure we negotiate effectively with our suppliers.'

'Our research clearly indicated that 83 per cent of small businesses feel they are not getting value from their law firms. This fact has underpinned our very high customer satisfaction metrics for our new lawyer service.'

The full version should still tell a story – again, remember it's taking the reader from a lack of interest and little understanding all the way to comprehension and enthusiasm. After you've prepared it, give it to someone who doesn't know your business and ask them the following questions after they've read it:

1. Do you understand what we do?
2. Does what we're doing sound credible?
3. Do you know how much we're raising and what we're going to do with the money?
4. Can you say how big our company will be in 3 years and 5 years?
5. Are you inclined to hear more?

In the full version, you may want to relegate complex slides to an appendix section and simply refer to them within the main body of the presentation. That way, you can keep the flow going and allow the reader to get the gist of what it's about in a relatively small number of 'pages'.

Remember, the full version is going to be read when you're not there to explain anything, so make everything very clear. You may have sent it to someone who's already expressed an interest, but they might have forwarded it to a friend or colleague for comment. You can't presume everyone who reads it will be supportive. Make sure, therefore, that all your claims are substantiated, and use language that is calm and factual:

Bad:

As early as year two, our innovative marketing campaign will project us ahead of our rivals in terms of customer numbers.

Better:

From year two onwards, our customer acquisition target of 45 per month should place us in line with, if not ahead of, published data from our identified competition.

The presented version can be far simpler in terms of content on each slide – in fact, the simpler the better. I like to challenge myself to give complete speeches with not one word on the whole deck. You may need a little practice to pull that off, and with that approach comes the difficulty of remembering all the facts you want to get over.

In practice, a balance is best. It's always good when presenting trends – whether industry, from your own business, or otherwise – to use charts and graphs. It brings the facts to life in a memorable way.[7]

Getting your communications ready – the teaser email and the executive summary

Before you're ready to run a campaign, you need to get all your 'sales' collateral together. That's a package of information that you will want to send to the prospective investors. The trick, as I'll repeat, is not to drown the investor, but to take them on a journey – from ignorance of you and your business idea, all the way through to enthusiasm and understanding.

The pack of information you'll need to send to investors is listed below, in the order you'll send it out:

1. Teaser email

2. Executive summary

3. Links to your organization's website and links to your 'home' page on the crowdfunding website

4. A promotional video

5. Financial plan

6. PowerPoint deck

7. Business or feasibility plan in Word

8. Cap table (the share history of the company)

If you decided not to use a crowdfunding company and fund entirely through angel investors, the next step would be subscription documents.

The sequence for a crowdfunding company is more like this:

1. The pack that the crowdfunding company will want to see when you engage them, including: business or feasibility plan to the crowdfunding company; cap table; financial plan; PowerPoint deck; executive summary; provisional investor list (your contacts, not theirs); details of your website

2. Supplementary information as you start to approach angel investors for the pre-funding: teaser email; promotional video

There will be a fuller list of information each crowdfunding company will require, but initially they will require what is listed above. Once you have engaged with them (i.e.

signed their contract), they will want to conduct what's known as due diligence. This is the process of validating your claims – such as 'we have processed 500 orders since we launched', or 'the market size for our idea is currently £150m in the UK', or 'I held the position of product manager at XYZ Limited', or even 'I have a first-class honours degree from Bristol University'.

Scripting, shooting and editing the video

Here are the key points again, as a reminder:

— Keep it to 3 minutes or less
— Like good television, keep the sentences short, clear and relevant
— Make it fun to watch – film in a setting that reinforces your story
— Script it along the lines of your exec summary – what's the problem, how prevalent is it, your solution, your plan to deliver that solution, what that means in terms of revenues, profits, and investment return for the video viewer, and finally a 'call to action' – what would they do after watching the video
— It needs to feature you, if you're leading the company or the fundraising
— It needs to have an endorsement, ideally from at least 2 people – who could be an existing investor and a customer who loves your company and its products

- It's not a pop video, so no flashy music to distract – but music can be used in the background

- But . . . production standards are important if you want to look professional – so don't wing it with your iPhone and iMovie editing software on your Mac

- Overall, it's about building trust – so work hard on looking honest, professional, sensible, and confident!

If you decide to get the video made professionally, but have no idea where to start finding someone to shoot it, then go on a number of crowdfunding sites, pick say five videos you like and then track down the production company.

Preparing the PR, social media and email messages

You'll want to be banging on about the same thing with the same facts in all media, but the 'tone of voice' will change.

Getting good PR reach is a challenge, but worth the effort. I wouldn't necessarily appoint a PR agency, but try to find a friend of a friend with some media connections. PR is a whole other book, and I can only give you some simple tips here.

PR has changed over the years. What used to be a focus on key journalists is now a focus on key 'influencers'; some of them might still be journalists, but they are often those who write blogs, podcast, or produce YouTube videos. It's not hard to find out who they are if you don't already know

– you can then use LinkedIn to get introduced, or other social media like Instagram and Facebook.

If I was doing the PR of a theatre company, for example, the message to the blogger might be:

> Hi Jane, Looks we might be the first theatre company in the UK to tackle the very real issues surrounding modern slavery – something dear to the heart of Mrs May. I'm still pinching myself – we've secured Kenneth Branagh to direct. Will drop you a media release in the morning when all this goes public – until then embargo please! Best regards, Julian

For general social media, keep the message short but have a relevant and arresting picture, plus a couple of links. A tweet might look like this:

> We've launched! XYZ Theatre Company's £50,000 crowdfunding campaign takes centre stage! Video at [shortened URL]. See how you can help at [shortened URL].

You can be more relaxed in your word count on Linked-In. Use the 'Write an article' feature. Again, use a great and relevant photo and make the text quite personal – after all, you're writing to someone in your own network:

> Dear friends,

> After many months of planning I'm pleased to announce that our campaign to raise funds for XYZ Company on Crowdfundco went live earlier today.

> We're raising £250,000 and would love you to get involved. Here's why . . .

We all love lawyers. We can't do without them. But legal services is one line item on our operating costs that always seems hard to control. Fees are still charged by the hour and the lawyers we use are nearly always based on a recommendation, regardless of whether the chosen lawyer is best for that specific task.

The legal services market is changing. A new breed of entrepreneurs has grown up without the baggage of tradition. They are negotiating everything, demanding value and using reverse auction platforms to buy services by getting suppliers to bid for their work. They are open to the idea that you 'buy at best' – meaning you only use the provider specifically fit for the task. XYZ saw this coming, and built an online marketplace matching businesses with our own unique nationwide panel of law firms keen to participate in competitive bidding to win your business. Works a treat.

Two years on and XYZ has demonstrated traction and market acceptance for the business model. Over 1200 requests have already passed through the system, with an estimated £1m's worth of bids.

The company is ready to scale, hence the fundraise. The money will be used primarily to ramp up customer acquisition. Both by online and offline targeting of SMEs, and by accelerating the already successful partnership programme.

I'm fairly sure you like disrupting as much as I do! XYZ is part of the next disruption: legal services. Watch this space. Or better still, jump on board. The train is leaving the station!

Creating your list of rewards and pricing them

So far we've not spoken about how to build a 'rewards' campaign. Rewards crowdfunding, as described in chapter 2, is the process of gaining money for your company without giving away shares. As such, it is far simpler and quicker, primarily because the regulations surrounding it are far less onerous. And that's because there's no investment involved. But there's still a need for a pre-campaign, so that the crowdfunding campaign gets off to a good start.

The success of a rewards campaign is very dependent upon approaching the right 'crowd'. Equity investment can appeal to anyone looking for investment return – so people invest in businesses that may be outside their knowledge base. But for rewards, you need people interested in what the reward is.

For example, if you're raising funds for a theatre project you need people who will be interested in and motivated to gain the relevant rewards.

In my theatre example, the rewards might be:

— A day at rehearsals

— Deeply discounted tickets for the duration of the run at the theatre

— Dinner/lunch with the producer, artistic director, writer, musical director, etc.

— Being named in credits as an executive producer

— Signed copies of the programme from the full cast

— Being named as a donor and supporter (even if there's no accompanying tangible reward)

— Invitation to first-night after-party

The crowd you need will govern which crowdfunding company to go for. It's a trade-off between crowdfunding companies with very large crowds and specialist crowdfunding companies where the crowd is smaller but the interest will be very high.

My advice is to follow the same selection criteria as you would for the equity crowdfunding companies, as will be discussed in chapter 6.

One last thing. Don't create too many rewards. Stick to 10 or 15 rewards maximum and price them sensibly. If you're raising £50,000, then work out how many of each reward you might reasonably sell to hit your goal. Make sure there are high-price and low-price rewards in the mix. Using my example above, the pricing might look like this:

— A day at rehearsals – 20 people per day at £50, over 5 days = £5,000

— Deeply discounted tickets for the duration of the run at the theatre – 250 ticket vouchers at £50 each = £12,500

— Dinner/lunch with the producer et al – 6 people per table @ £250 each, over 10 days = £15,000

— Being named in credits as an executive producer = 5 people @ £1,000 = £5,000

— Signed copies of the programme from the full cast – 250 at £20 each = £5,000

— Being named as a donor and supporter – 250 people @ £10 each = £2,500

— Invitation to first-night after-party – 50 people at £250 each = £12,500

This gives a grand total of £57,500 (to ensure target of £50,000 is reached).

Creating visuals and graphics (required with a rewards campaign)

Selling your rewards is massively helped by good images or graphics. Some crowdfunding companies are very good at creating the graphics for you. But really, anyone could do it. Just make sure they all look like they fit together in design terms. Keep them simple and in black and white. They can have wording at the foot – like DONOR, AFTER-PARTY or SIGNED PROG BY CAST, etc.

Branding

What are your brand values? Why are they important, even for a start-up?

You'd think that, when raising funds, you and your colleagues in the company would need to do no more than look presentable. The investors are primarily investing in the business idea; they want to know you'll deliver the plan professionally.

We need to keep going back to what tips an investor 'over the edge', so that he or she says 'yes' to investing, and a big factor in that is trust. You have to be able to do the following:

— Look professional

— Communicate what you do effectively

— Be convincing about your investment proposition

— Speak intelligently

— Be knowledgeable about your industry

— Work well as a team

— Keep your promises

— Inspire confidence that you'll deliver the results

— Make the investor respect, or even like you

— Engage the investor, so they're proud to be associated with your project

The list could go on. But did you notice that many of these attributes and skills apply in the advertising industry when selling a product? Of course, the process marketers use to wrap all that up is the brand.

This is my formula:

BRAND = PERSONALITY + PROMISE

The PROMISE is what you do, and the PERSONALITY is the way you deliver it.

Both Ryanair and EasyJet deliver a PROMISE. They fly people in an aeroplane to other parts of the world. The PERSONALITY is the way in which they do this. It's the look and feel of the company, the way the staff behave, the way the experience makes you feel about yourself. But above all, it's the degree of engagement you feel with the organization. Do you want to be associated with them and sing their praises? What does being an EasyJet or Ryanair customer say about you?

In my lectures at business school I always show the following.

BRAND = PERSONALITY + PROMISE

PC = Personality (dull, lacking in innovation, follower, let's me down) + **Promise** (cheap, wide choice)

MAC = Personality (cool, new ideas, young, designerish) + **Promise** (reliable, easy to use, virus free)

OK, perhaps that's a little unfair on the humble PC, but you get the idea. Once you know that the effect you want to achieve is delivered through 'brand consciousness', then the 'tool kit' separating out Promise and Personality allows you to ensure that you're strong in the elemental parts – which then come together to form your brand.

In practical terms, here's what you need to do in relation to your team and your pitch to investors:

PROMISE

— Objective industry research that supports your proposition that the idea will succeed

— Evidence of traction

— A costed-out business model with factual information – including sensible cash requirements

— An investment proposition that is attractive

— Skills and experience of the team as proof that you are capable of delivering on the plan

PERSONALITY

— Can-do attitude

— Intelligent demeanour

— Honest and trustworthy

— Responsive and helpful

— Funny, engaging, likeable characters

— Give off a sense that working with you would be fun and rewarding

— Professional approach

I suggest you have a look at yourselves beyond how you dress for meetings. Try and pull apart the two elements of your brand and make sure you can deliver most of what you want to project.

There's much more reading you can do about this subject – and the best place to start searching is around the idea of the brand pyramid. A brand pyramid is a graphic representation of a brand. By discussing and defining each layer of the pyramid, you'll build up to a core 'essence' – the simple definition of what you and your business are all about. In Appendix III, Lucian Camp, a branding expert and former creative director of top London agencies, guides you through further definitions of a brand and gives you the step-by-step process for building the brand pyramid of your own company.

Creating a simple website for your company or project

It's easy to find a company to build you a website. If you already have one, then create what's known as a 'landing page'. This is a dedicated page within your website relating to the funding campaign. Promote the URL to your prospective investors and it will be that page they see first. You can restate the investment pitch on the landing page and then lead them off to other parts of your website as required. Dropping them straight onto your home page loses the continuity of your story and the journey you are taking them on.

Who's in charge here? Choosing your team and rewarding them

I could fill another book with advice about surrounding yourself with the right team. The focus here is on ensuring effective management, good decision-making, and overall competence.

When I ask who's in charge here, I mean who's driving both the company and the fundraising? I come across great executives, fresh from business schools, and they still have a 'study group' mentality, as if they're trained to only work collegiately. My advice is that every great company or organization needs an unchallenged, strong leader. Before you do any presentations – even informal ones over a laptop in a Starbucks – get your act together as to who's driving the meeting and who's making the ultimate decisions.

I have been criticized in the past for my uncompromising attitude towards team members. If there are one or more weak members of the team, they've got to go. And go ASAP. It's a corny and well-voiced cliché, but people invest in people. I personally believe that most investors buy into a great idea and then decide if the management is capable of delivering that idea's potential. What's certainly true is that an unimpressive team member can kill a potential investment. Remember, most angel investors are successful business people and used to judging the competence and deliverability of their executives. Yes, weak team members can be trained, or remotivated, or taught better presentation skills, but you don't have time to carry baggage. Fundraising is not easy, and running an enterprise is even harder. How do you get rid of them? Simply say you've given it some thought and you're not confident that they're right fit for the team. Blunt is good. If they have shares in the business, then use an impartial adviser or mentor to resolve the terms of their exit.

Having said all this, what if you don't have a team yet? How do you go about putting one together? The statistic from the crowdfunding companies is that you will raise about 70 per cent more if you are a team of 4 than you would on your own. Obviously don't just co-opt someone to make up the numbers; think through who might complement your skills in the context of what you're doing. If you are skilled at administration, project management and the detail, why not look for someone who is good at sales and marketing? Don't find a group of personal clones.

Reality check

Preparation is hard and lengthy – still want to go ahead?

It's always good to take stock of where you are in your thinking. The good news is that if you've followed everything up to now and feel you've been able to put everything into motion along the lines we've shared, then it's plain sailing from here on out.

6:

PLANNING THE CAMPAIGN

How do I get started?

Clear your diary – this could be a long haul! My greatest respect goes to the entrepreneur. Any entrepreneur. It's a kind of benign madness to give up secure employment and set out on your own.

Not everyone has the choice. Family and/or money obligations may stop you starting your own business. Over the last fifteen years, universities have continued to turn out highly employable people, but there haven't been the jobs for them to go to. Many graduates have stayed in education, adding an MA or MSc to their first degree, and a subset of those have brought forward their planned time at business school, hoping the tough times will have passed by the end of their MBA.

But if there's a single positive driving factor that made the label 'entrepreneur' acceptable, it's the phenomenal success of mega-companies facilitated by the internet. Examples include Larry Page and Sergey Brin's Google, Jeff Bezos's Amazon, Pierre Omidyar's eBay, Mark Zuckerberg's Facebook, Mark Cuban's Yahoo, Ma Huateng's Tencent, Jack Ma's Alibaba and Peter Thiel's PayPal. It's not just the companies that have inspired – their founders have become the new rock stars.

What they all have in common is a passion to make

things better, cheaper, faster and more efficient, or, as is the case with Facebook, enable you to do something not even contemplated before their existence. Truly changing society.

So whatever's driving you, hang in there. If there's a valid reason for your business or project to exist, then you'll stay motivated and others will support you in making it happen.

Clearing the diary? Absolutely. And by that, I mean get yourself organized to be able to devote pretty much all of your time to this process – and that's just the fundraising. Tell your partner, friends, or others you're close to that it will mean time in the project office, late nights, frustrations. They may not like the new you. Just keep telling yourself it's worth it and never, ever, give up until all appears lost. Then tweak your idea and start again.

Clearing the diary also means no distractions. I know some people have to keep making money while they moonlight on the new business, but investors want to see 110 per cent passion and commitment. Do try to clear about six months to allow you the time to make it all work. The rewards in terms of personal esteem are really worth it. Trust me.

Choosing the right crowdfunding service partner

In theory, it's easy. You find the one that's delivered more success than others and go with them.

But, having run a number of crowdfunding campaigns now, I know it's not that simple.

Here's my list of key considerations for choosing a crowd-funding company:

- What campaigns have they successfully run for businesses or projects like yours? That means your market sector, your size, your level of funding, and your stage of development. Crowdfunding companies promise the earth because they want to 'win' your project, but only hard facts work for me. What you want is some comparability. If they normally do £500,000 for tech start-ups and you're looking for £50,000 for a theatre project, they may take you on but they're not really going to bust a gut to make your fundraising a success.

- How big is their crowd? How many active investors do they have? How do they define active investor? Is that someone who has invested at some stage or someone who has invested recently? Or someone who has invested, say, 5 times over the last year? Who is their crowd? Is it a relevant list of committed investors or just thousands of general consumers wanting to have a punt like they would on a horse race? You won't get general punters to back a complex new algorithm for data security any more than you'll get committed semi-professional investors to back your 'party bags for kids' idea.

- What will they do for you? That means how much assistance they offer at the planning stage on, perhaps, the level of funding you should go for, and how they will promote your project on and offline. Will they, for example, give assistance in editing your copy, scripting your video or crafting messages to investors throughout the campaign?

- Do you think they're professional? The key here will be the project person they allocate to you. Crowdfunding companies tend to employ good sales people to hook you, but don't let you get near the analysts and legal team until you're committed – yet it's those people that make or break the campaign. Try and hold all your meetings at their offices. What impression do they create? Organized and process-driven or a bit flaky?

- What's the process and timescale? Are they helping you to understand all the stages you'll go through? Are they glossing over key details, like legal compliance? When you ask for a project timescale with landmark dates are they compliant with your request? Are they pushing you to launch at a time of their own choosing (when their business is flat) like Christmas or the middle of the summer holidays? Some companies have prepared good booklets – ask if they have one.

- Funnily enough, what it will cost me is way down my list of priorities. You're going to pay around 6 per cent – they all charge pretty much the same. But there are ways to get the fees down – see later in this chapter.

- Overall, I want to know if they think my fundraising will succeed. For all the chit-chat, you'll just have to plump for the one that sounds the most credible, understands your business immediately and appears to really want to work hard for you.

Tip: Choose the crowdfunding company using these simple steps:

1. Do desk research. Quickest route to the very latest list of good crowdfunding companies can be found by Googling 'Crowdfunding companies in the UK'.

2. Pick five that look relevant.

3. Invest a small amount (£10 will do) with each of the five by choosing companies to back that are almost at 100 per cent funded and nearing the end of the campaigns – that way you learn how they handle you from the other side, and you see how good they are post-investment, too.

4. Find someone, a mentor, or business friends, to accompany you to all the meetings. Even if you have a team, an experienced mentor is a useful addition at meetings – they lend gravitas and can 'appear' to give reasoned, independent opinion on what you're saying.

5. Make a list of your key criteria before you go.

6. Go and see each. And mark them against your key criteria for selection.

7. Go back to the top two companies and say you're inclined to work with them. BUT . . . tell them the name of the other company you're considering.

They may tell you something you don't know about the alternative, but it may also tell you something about their ethics and professionalism if they compliment or slag-off their rival.

8. Pick the one you want and ask to see their contract. Get the friend/mentor to review it and don't be shy of going back and asking questions or getting changes to the agreement. If you can't get what you want, switch to the other company. Don't drop your number two choice until you're contracted to your number one.

What will a crowdfunding company do for you?

As I've already said, all crowdfunding companies will do the basic job of cajoling you to get your information pack into good shape and processing you through the compliance.

But it will be helpful for you to know what they won't do – or only do reluctantly!

— Make decisions for you as to how much funding you need

— Comment or advise on the viability of your business or project plan

— Tell you at an early stage if their compliance team is 'likely' to be OK with what you've submitted in draft

— Share with you anything about the amount of pre-funding you should secure

— Share with you details about other campaigns they've run and why they succeeded or failed

— Tell you anything helpful during the campaign that they will do unilaterally to increase the probability of your campaign succeeding (it's all up to you, it seems!)

Negotiating the agreement and the fees

The contracts will be fairly standard, but one key point you should try and negotiate is to not pay fees on investors you bring along. These will be the investors in the pre-funding round (See chapter 1) who you will have secured to kick-off your campaign. The catch is that the crowdfunding companies will say that any investor who invests through their platform must be subject to fees. But your pre-campaign investors are only going through the platform to build the momentum that will bring in the investors the crowdfunding company attracts. Have a go at what's called a carve out. This means you agree a list of your own investors who, if they invest, their investment amounts will be 'carved out' from the final total on which the crowdfunding company's fees will be based. If you can't get them down to 0 per cent then settle for 3 per cent, which would be 50 per cent of their fee rate.

You might also ask for 'most favoured nation' terms. This obligates the crowdfunding company to offer you a fee rate which is no worse than anyone else, or, if you can swing it, no higher than the lowest rate any client of theirs has paid.

If they think you're a prestigious project or one that will

easily succeed, they'll be more inclined to negotiate. Remember, you can bluff as much as you want, but in the end you need them – so no bravado! No walking away with an 'I'll show them who's boss' mentality!

Creating and managing the list of investors you want to approach

A great entrepreneurial friend, Xavier Azalbert, once said, 'when it comes to fundraising you have to be humble'. You may have been very senior in your past life, but being an entrepreneur means going back to the end of the queue in terms of status. If there's ever a moment to beg, it's now!

To call yourself genuinely ready to launch a funding campaign, you and your colleagues, if you are working in a team, need an extensive list of contacts to approach. In practice, given that you want 30 per cent of your target as pre-funding, you need to work back from that figure and do some probability calculations. Get this wrong, and come in at 5 per cent or 10 per cent of target after pre-funding, and you risk failure. Having said that, large crowdfunding companies don't seem to agree. Seedrs say you need 30 per cent to give yourself near to 100 per cent probability,[8] yet Crowdcube say that even 5 per cent can be OK. The message appears to be play safe and secure as much as you can beforehand – don't leave it to chance.

There are a number of types of people or organizations you should have on your list.

1. People you know who have invested in businesses before.

2. Well-connected friends, or friends of friends, who are willing to forward your approach email and executive summary.

3. Agents – that's individuals and small consultancies who do fundraising for fees. There are so many it's hard to list.

4. Existing customers – it's always a good ploy to approach those you know, and who by definition like what you do as a business. Just be sure that you announcing you're looking to raise money won't surprise them – it could give the impression your company or project is at risk of stopping if you fail to raise the money.

5. Suppliers. Be careful here – you don't want a conflict of interest. But keeping them to a small percentage shouldn't be too hard.

6. Professionals. This would include your firm of accountants, and perhaps your law firm if you've used one for a while. I have to say this is rarely an effective route, as they are constrained by the FCA (Financial Conduct Authority) as to how far they can promote your fundraising to their clients.

7. Then you have social media. If you're an avid user of LinkedIn, Instagram, Twitter or Facebook, there may be someone out there in media land whose imagination you can catch.

8. You could add small family offices – these are professional investing organizations set up by affluent families to manage their wealth. It would be very rare to get at them cold, but if you have a

connection you could approach them. They sometimes make an exception and put small amounts into businesses, with a view that if the business starts to do well, they can 'follow on' with a larger amount at the next round (i.e. the next fundraising stage of your business).

9. Lastly, there's friends and family. You may already have approached them at an early stage of your enterprise and their enthusiasm may be strong but their pockets too shallow to go the next stage. As we'll discuss later, very often a 'yes' decision from an investor is emotional, sometimes as simple as them liking you and trusting you without fully understanding the risks. Should you fail, you might claim you acted reasonably in sharing the information, so nothing should come as a surprise, but it would be unfair to imply it's a friend or relative's fault if they haven't read the detail. Even if it's true. You may feel it's a step too far to risk the money of family and close friends – they will have trusted you not to let them down and won't necessarily have done their homework.

There's an example of how you might want to format your list in the figure overleaf. As you can see, it's very logical – a list of people by name, whose contact they are, who is 'owning' them in terms of follow-up, their classification (angel, fund, accountant, etc.), multiple columns to allow for the date and detail of what they've been successively sent, a status column to annotate with their reaction and actions arising – like 'promised to send them a copy of an industry report'.

Campaign planner

Name	Whose contact?	Phone	Email	Email shot	Exec summary	Response 1
John Smith	me	07712345678	XX@example.com	01-Jan-18	01-Jan-18	no thanks
Kate Evans	me	07712345678	XX@example.com	01-Jan-18	01-Jan-18	06-Jan-18
Peter White	JL	07712345678	XX@example.com	01-Jan-18	01-Jan-18	06-Jan-18
Jane Brown	me	07712345678	XX@example.com	01-Jan-18	01-Jan-18	no thanks
Mike Depp	PS	07712345678	XX@example.com	01-Jan-18	01-Jan-18	06-Jan-18
Amy Bevan	nm	07712345678	XX@example.com	01-Jan-18	01-Jan-18	07-Jan-18

	Financial pack+PPT	Response 2	Response 3	Notes
John Smith	-	-	-	Active angel backed XYZ co in 2011
Kate Evans	06-Jan-18	mtg 20 jan	Yes £20k	Knows our sector - active angel
Peter White	06-Jan-18	mtg 21 jan	Yes £30k	Co-invested with JS already
Jane Brown	-	-	-	Long shot - old contact
Mike Depp	06-Jan-18	no thanks	-	Slow to decide but a possibility
Amy Bevan	07-Jan-18	mtg 23 jan	no thanks	Mostly backs media projects

This spreadsheet is very dynamic, in that it can be continuously updated. And make sure you note how 'No' their 'No' is! A 'No' might simply mean, 'I'm very busy at the moment, so if you need a quick answer, I'll have to say no.' This needs noting, so that when the crowdfunding campaign starts you can go back to these people with an appropriately targeted message, like, 'I know you indicated you were busy a few weeks ago, but I just wanted to share that the crowdfunding campaign has now gone live. Why not follow this link, and see if you'd like to come on board as an investor?'

Other stuff to get ready

Here's a summary that should form a checklist for you as you embark on your campaign.

Once you have your 'sales collateral' together (that's the two-page exec summary, the financial model, the Power-

Point 'deck', and the Cap Table), submit it to the crowd-funding company ASAP. So they can start the due diligence. This can run in parallel to you going out to win pre-campaign pledges from individual investors.

Check with your accountant or lawyer (or a knowledge-able friend) if you are SEIS or EIS compliant. This means your investors will be able to claim various tax benefits if they invest. If you've not submitted an application to HMRC, then do so as soon as possible. You'll want to tell investors you are compliant – not just that you've applied.

Have you formed a company? If you're encouraging investment then you're going to need one. It's very cheap and simple, and is done at www.gov.uk/limited-company-formation/setting-up.

If you've already formed a company, you'll have articles of association – basically the formal document lodged in the public domain with Companies House. You might also have a shareholders' agreement, which sits in parallel to the articles and sets out what you and other shareholders agree between you as regards, for example, who gets to go on your board, and what happens if one of the shareholders wants to sell their shares. Nowadays, the key terms of a sharehold-ers' agreement are often embedded into the single document of the Articles. Crowdfunding companies prefer this, as it reassures the smaller investor that everything is open and transparent.

Do you have a contract of employment with your own company? You need one. Investors want to know that you're 'locked in'. No one wants to invest in a management team only to find they decide to walk out should things get tough.

Do you have a cap table ready? This is a list of the share-holders you might have already and how many shares they have. I've included an example below. It might be that you are the sole shareholder with one share. In which case, you might want to split the shares into 1,000 shares, or even 1,000,000 shares. This makes it easy to allocate small packets of shares to investors who are only investing small amounts. The cap table allows you to illustrate what the shareholder list will look like after the investment round or crowd campaign has closed.

CAP TABLE

Round 1 (date 1)

	Investment	Price per share £	Shares Issued	Total shares	% of equity held
John Smith	70,000	1.00	70,000	70,000	28%
Jane Glover	60,000	1.00	60,000	60,000	24%
Peter Orient	50,000	1.00	50,000	50,000	20%
James Clark	40,000	1.00	40,000	40,000	16%
Jenny Green	30,000	1.00	30,000	30,000	12%
	250,000		250,000	250,000	100%

Round 2 (date 2)

	Investment	Price per share £	Shares Issued	Total shares	% of equity held
John Smith	50,000	1.50	33,333	103,333	23%
Jane Glover	50,000	1.50	33,333	93,333	21%
Peter Orient	30,000	1.50	20,000	70,000	16%
James Clark	40,000	1.50	26,667	66,667	15%
Jenny Green	30,000	1.50	20,000	50,000	11%
Ben Allright	100,000	1.50	66,667	66,667	15%
	300,000		200,000	450,000	100%

Share all your documents with a friend, mentor or another businessperson you know, starting with the executive summary. Ask them if, having read it, they understand what your company/idea is all about, how much money you are raising and the deal for the investor, how they feel about the proposition – i.e. would they be inclined to take a call from you or have a meeting? Are they interested? – and lastly, is it clear what they should do next, or what will happen next? Obviously if you miss the mark on any of this, you need to go back and make some changes.

Create a list of all the investors you know. That's absolutely everyone you've come in contact with! Get their names and email addresses only – that's all you'll need. Use the EBAN website (www.eban.org – the European Trade Association for Business Angels, Seed Funds and Early Stage Market Players) to find a list of all the angel investor clubs in the UK. Approach the clubs and ask how to register with them.

Sign on with LinkedIn and Facebook, and set up a dedicated Twitter account for the business, separate from your personal one. You're going to use these social media to raise funds, and to push the crowdfunding campaign once it starts.

It really helps to have a website. Investors will read all your investment docs – but they also like to see what your customers see. And they like to mystery shop. That means they like to go online, see if the website works, absorb the style and culture of your business and generally see how user-friendly the experience is. If they like what they see, it will give them confidence you're going to be effective at running the business. If you're at a very early stage you can have a small website with a message on it – perhaps not quite as simple as 'coming soon' – but one that says what you do as an organization, and gives contact details.

You can start the approach to the crowdfunding companies in parallel to all these activities. But you'll be in a stronger position to engage productively and quickly with them if you've already started to secure your pre-investor commitments. So start with what you've got and get out there selling. See chapter 7 on how to run that pre-campaign.

Due diligence and compliance

If there's a likely moment of frustration, it will be when your crowdfunding company starts due diligence.

To be fair, the FCA (Financial Conduct Authority) has quite rightly stepped into this peer-to-peer marketplace to ensure investors are protected and that there is an orderly process. For this reason, all crowdfunding companies are regulated by the FCA (it's still wise to just check on their website that they state: Regulated by the Financial Conduct Authority).

However, such is the fear of further regulation among the crowdfunding community, that I've sensed an over-cautious approach, bordering on obsession, when it comes to them checking facts about your business!

Basically, the Due Diligence (DD) process is to verify every claim you make. There are some examples below.

I was CEO of ABC Limited from July 2014 to September 2016

DD will require evidence that you were a director of that company, evidence you were appointed as CEO, and Companies House records as to when you were appointed to the board and resigned from it. Press coverage won't do. Nor will letters from your lawyer. Nor will a written reference from someone still at ABC Limited.

We sold the XYZ Company Limited business in 2015

DD will require a copy of the sale and purchase agreement.

The processed meatball market in the UK is worth £450m per annum

DD will want a reference to the research document from which that claim is taken, and it will need to be official. A Bloomberg report won't do, but a government report on the state of the UK processed foods market will be acceptable.

The trick here is to see this coming and start to gather evidence as you go along. It will save days of delays and frustration.

There are loopholes. Anything that comes out from the crowdfunding company must be checked and passed by them. But paradoxically, anything you say or give to an investor outside that 'umbrella' is free of regulation. What you give your pre-campaign investors is up to you, and even if a crowdfunding-sourced investor asks you a question, what you reply is not under the auspices of the regulatory rules. Mad, but true.

This compliance process is not a bad discipline for you to work within. After all, it's really just telling the truth at all times, not misleading investors and bearing in mind that substantiated facts will always trump hype when building trust.

7:

GOING LIVE!

Running the 'pre-campaign' – how to get the essential 33 per cent

Here's how to hit your target amount of pre-funding before launching the crowdfunding campaign:

Gather a master list of everyone you know and, if you're working in a team or with friends, everyone they know. Get it onto a spreadsheet. If you're familiar with Dropbox or Google Docs, then set up a shared file which everyone can update.

Make your column headers defined steps in the process – like 'send teaser email and Exec Summary', 'send follow-up chaser email', 'send info pack', and include a comment column for each.

Send out your teaser emails with a common core, but top and tail each with a personalized message.

The core might look like:

Arguably, the way we all buy legal services needs a shake up, and XYZ got its reverse-auction platform up around 2 years ago. We already have credible traction in terms of revenue and platform traffic.

Have a look at the investment video, and the attached executive summary, and let me know if you can participate, either by investing in your own right or by suggesting someone who might. I'll send you a pack of information and details of the investment return when you're ready.

With personalization, it will look like this:

Hi [their first name]

We haven't spoken for a while. Trust all is well? It must be over a year now since we last met!

Not sure what your appetite is at the moment for new investments. But I thought this one might appeal!

As you probably know I've started a great company called XYZ Limited and I'm raising £250,000 in a funding round. I'm looking for around £100,000 from investors such as yourself, with the balance coming from a planned crowdfunding campaign that will go live in a couple of months.

Arguably, the way we all buy legal services needs a shake up, and XYZ got its reverse-auction platform up around 2 years ago. We already have credible traction in terms of revenue and platform traffic.

Have a look at the investment video, and the attached executive summary, and let me know if you can participate, either by investing in your own right or by suggesting someone who might. I'll send you a pack of information and details of the investment return when you're ready.

I'd really appreciate your feedback too.

Thanks, and speak soon.

Best wishes,

[your first name]

If you're just getting commitments to invest, try and button them down quickly. If you get a 'buy' signal, such as 'this looks interesting, I've got a few questions', then arrange to meet. Don't just send the pack. Or rather, arrange to meet but send the pack a short time ahead of the meeting. It's easier to deal with concerns or objections talking face to face.

If the reply email says, 'no thanks' or the classic, 'not for me', ask why they're not interested. It could be they are fully invested, or they don't invest in your sector, or they are too busy with other projects. All reasonable objections. But if they say, 'your sales figures look too ambitious', or 'I've seen a plan like this already and it failed', or 'a friend of mine says this is a bad sector to invest in', then politely ask if you can have a meeting anyway. If they say no thanks, then try and keep the door open with comments like: 'OK, but if we look as if we're going to be successful in raising all the funds, then I'll come to you, if I may, to see if you want to change your mind.' Or, 'I was rather hoping you'd give me a bit of your time to look through the numbers and critique the model.' Either way, you're not letting them shut down the line of communication.

If they express interest or decline, then your next set of actions is the same. Keep them in the loop! This means sending out updates of your progress. If you're already in business and have Google Analytics to share (page views on your website, unique user numbers, etc.), then send those out at regular intervals – even weekly. Or if you sign a new customer, share that news. Really anything that reinforces the notion in the prospective investor's head that 'hey, maybe this is worth getting involved with'.

One of the strongest incentives to invest is what I call the 'train is leaving the station, do you want to get on board?' approach. Every time an investor says yes, ask if you can share their name with other prospective investors. And share the implications of that investment: 'now that John Smith has come on board with a £15,000 commitment, we are 65 per cent of the way towards our pre-funding goal'.

Always ask for a referral. As you've seen in the teaser email, it's good practice to ask if they know someone else who might be interested. There are two reasons to do this. One is that investors almost always hunt in packs. They will co-invest with other investors and like to share interesting companies across their network. The other reason is that they have more 'trust momentum' with a third party than you do. If I get a personal recommendation from a fellow investor, I nearly always take the time to read the business plan.

And don't forget other key activities at this stage. Sending out regular messages on your social media pages from you and your inner circle. It can be a good-news stream, or it can be more direct. You might announce that a group of interested investors are meeting and ask if anyone else would like to come along.

This latter technique is also effective if someone fears being 'sold to'. I call it 'mezzanine selling'. Instead of asking to meet them, suggest that a group of investors are meeting and would they like to join them. When I've used mezzanine selling, no one felt under pressure personally and I could answer challenging questions there and then – the converts within your audience also spread confidence and encouragement to the waverers.

There's no substitute to picking up the phone and chatting to people. If they know you directly they should take your call. If you don't know them directly, then get the person you have in common to suggest a call. Most people are reasonable and inclined to help, so be courageous. It's your future in the balance here. Be brave!

You may think during this phase of your campaign that pitching to angel clubs is a laborious and perhaps ineffective use of your time. Not so. Firstly, even one investor gained after a drive from Birmingham to Cambridge for the day is time well spent. If nothing else, the more you pitch to angels, the more confident you will get in presenting and in handling the Q&A session at the end of your talk. These will be fairly sophisticated investors, and from my experience their feedback will be invaluable at tuning your pitch, let alone helping you to realize the weaknesses in your proposition that you can go away and fix.

All the way through, share the feedback across your team or helpers. What you learn will be helpful to them when approaching investors too.

During this time, you will have progressed your planning with the crowdfunding company and will be able to tell your pre-funding investors how this is going to work. They will be asked to make their pledges on the crowdfunding website and you will be able to guide them when they do that. The FCA clamped down on multiple investments from the same person, as it misled investors into thinking the number of people investing was larger than it was. Now, each investor must pledge their intended amount in one go.

How to nudge an investor into a 'yes' decision

You'd think once someone has agreed to invest, that getting him or her to actually go online to the crowdfunding website and invest would be simple!

But the reality is that it takes a big nudge to push them over the edge and commit. Some of the reluctance might be excusable, particularly if they have an alternative demand on their funds. But the hesitation could arise from a lack of the good news about your company they were expecting, or simply a slow draining away of enthusiasm from the high point when they said 'yes'.

Another obstacle is the crowdfunding websites themselves. An investor has to register with the crowdfunding company, they have to define themselves in terms of their sophistication as an investor, and then they must key in the pledge and fill in their debit card details. (Note its debit card, not credit card.) All of which is far from easy or enjoyable, in user-experience terms. The debit card aspect spooks many people, as they assume the money will be taken from the bank account immediately; especially troubling for them if they are pledging more than the amount of funds currently in their account. Often an investor will have registered some time before, perhaps with a different email address and password. The result is that the system refuses to accept a new registration.

There's very little you can do, other than to clearly set out what will happen for each investor, perhaps like this:

- Go onto the website and familiarize yourself with our section and all the data we've uploaded to assist you.

- You can ask us questions through the website to clarify any points, or to allay any concerns you have.

- Once you're ready to pledge, register with the crowdfunding company. They'll ask you some simple questions, which are essential for investor protection. Please be patient – everyone has to jump over the same hurdles!

- As soon as you're registered, you can make your pledge. You kindly indicated you were prepared to invest £5,000, and that's the figure you should key into the appropriate box when asked.

- You'll be asked for your **debit** card details – crowdfunding platforms can't take payments from a credit card, as will be explained below . . .

- Don't worry! You might be concerned that the money will leave your account straight away. It won't. If the campaign is unsuccessful, no money will be taken from your account. If, after the end of the allotted time (30 days, for example), the campaign has reached its target, you will be given a further 2 weeks in which to change your mind before the money will be taken from your account.

- Please make sure you have enough funds in your account at that stage. Again, don't worry; you'll be guided all the way via emails.

- Lastly, to get our campaign off to a flying start, I'd welcome you pledging your money ASAP. Early indications of investor enthusiasm have a big impact on a campaign gathering momentum

- And if you have any queries please contact John Smith at Crowdfundco on this number and they'll help immediately. Or, if you prefer, just ring me on +44 1234 567 899.

- Thanks again for your support – we really look forward to having you with us.

Answering all the due diligence questions

This is required when selling shares, and in practice it's recommended that you deal with investor questions openly. By that, I mean if one investor emails back and says, for example, 'what happens to your sales figures if the STG/EURO exchange rate changes significantly, won't you lose customers?' Prepare your answer and send it to all the investors you've started a dialogue with. You might ask, 'Why share a problem?' But it works to your advantage if all investors see you've already thought of that issue and have a good answer.

Boosting your PR with a webinar

You may want to follow up the video with a studio discussion. Not necessarily at the pre-funding stage, but when the crowdfunding campaign has started. For example, we ran a campaign for the company LawyerFair. It was a low-cost, streamed webinar from Steve Hyland's studios at Business Connections Live TV, in west London. We promoted the time and date on social media and through the crowdfunding communications channels, and took live questions during the programme. Then we sent a link out after to ensure everyone saw it. It didn't replace the video, but offered a supplementary Q&A and due diligence process to those investors on the path to investing. It cost about £1,500, but you do get a video that can form part of your follow-up pack for investors.

Picking the right campaign launch date

Given that the campaigns normally last 30 days (although you can haggle for an extension if you look as if you need it), you'll want to ensure both the start and finish are in peak 'business' seasons – that's mid-January to a week or so before Easter, and again starting from late September through to early December. Try and avoid school holidays and empty-nester holiday times too (when adults without children or with grown-up children take early autumn holidays).

Don't get rushed into taking a date that you're uncomfortable with. Remember, you're in control!

Organizing the kick-off launch event, and another for mid-campaign

Just a reminder here that creating a bit of a PR stir at the start of the campaign, and as it gains momentum, will work wonders. It can be simple. Pick a room in London, or wherever you're based, that feels full with around 35–50 people.

Here's a general guide:

- Choose a venue that is on brand. You're an app developer? Head for a venue in your nearest tech district. You're a maker of natural scented candles? Perhaps hire-out an organic cafe close to a park or in the countryside.

- Pick a date near to or just into the start of your crowdfunding campaign, but make sure it's at least 6 weeks away – any sooner and invitees' diaries might be full. Make sure beforehand that key potential investors (and of course your team) are free on that evening.

- Prepare an attractive and professional invitation that you can send both digitally and physically.

- Invite for an after-work time of around 6 p.m., with a 7 p.m. start and a 7.30 finish for the presentations, and then a wrap-up time of about 8.30. Don't delay the start if there are still a few guests still to arrive – it's very discourteous to those who arrived on time. Have lots of drinks for the after period, when people are networking.

- Have a couple of presentations. Perhaps the two or more that appear in the video. Have a short one from an endorser – 5 mins – at the start. Then you or the project leader can do a snappy 10 mins. Then someone from the crowdfunding company could perhaps explain how to invest through their platform.

- Needless to say, arrive early and test everything out – AV equipment, your laptop, the lighting, the room setting of chairs, the temperature, and the logistics of name badges, meeting and greeting and dealing with late arrivals if you've started presenting, etc.

Tip: This is 90 per cent about building trust and coming over as professional, and 10 per cent about the investment proposition.

Organizing your team – who's doing what?

It's a tough and perhaps unwelcome thing to say, but the group of people you're working with on your project may not be able to 'grow' in capability as you progress. If you can recognize this now, then my advice is to deal with it sooner rather than later. Once your business has taken off, it's much harder to get rid of someone not up to the task, or who is simply not pulling his or her weight.

But, assuming you have a great, supportive team or perhaps just a good small group of advisers, then you need to assign them roles.

If you've reached the stage when your funding campaign is ready to go live, then the really hard work is done. But, nevertheless, assign the tasks as evenly as you can. These will be:

— Liaising with the crowdfunding company at the top level and being the gatekeeper

— Liaising with your existing shareholders, your lawyers and the crowdfunding company's lawyers, as well as other professional providers

- Gathering and preparing the 'stream of good news' and orchestrating its dissemination direct to investors and through social media

- Keeping track of outgoing emails to investors and their responses

- Allocating who should follow up each request for more information and organizing meetings and phone calls in response

- Organizing the events (if you do them) and making them happen

- Minding the shop – it should be business as usual through all this, so keep selling or doing what's necessary to show investors you're making it happen

Make me a deal – choosing the right investors

Although, in theory, you don't need to worry about the shape of the final deal to all investors until you're haggling with them, in practice it's a key part of getting investor-ready.

My advice is the same that I give relating to the preparation of a CV. Every CV should be bespoke for the organization you are applying to join. It should be tailored to present you in the best light, and to show your specific relevance to that organization.

And so it is with investors. At the early stages of a funding campaign, you need to think through what you want.

Obviously, you want the investor's money, but what else? Here's a list to give you some ideas:

— Strong know-how of your business sector

— High profile in your sector, so that other investors will be reassured/impressed

— Well connected – in terms of industry contacts, and in terms of linking you to other potential investors

— Evidence of effectiveness at board level – i.e. already served as a non-exec director before, or as a chairperson. This means they have a thorough understanding of company law, especially relating to board protocols and legal obligations relating to Companies House filings

— Good at working in a team – strong collegiate temperament, as opposed to being someone who would, in different circumstances, want to run your business

— Experience at building a company of your scale before, and perhaps experience of selling a business either via a trade sale (selling to a company that wants to buy you), or an IPO (an Initial Public Offering on the stock market).

By thinking this through, you can then make a proposition to a number of potential investors who would complement each other. Not everyone, for example, needs to be strong on financial accounting and reporting.

In this way, you can target an investor with a specific deal. For example, 'we're looking for six investors each investing £25,000 and we'd welcome you, as you have such strong skills in financial management.' In chapter 6 we looked at all the other factors you should consider when choosing who to target, and how to go about contacting them, but at this stage of your planning you can just give thought to what you need and what your ideal investor group would look like.

Staying close to your crowdfunding service company

There's a tendency for crowdfunding companies to set you up and walk away, leaving all the marketing, administration and effort of making the campaign successful up to you.

The better ones will set up regular calls to check on progress, take stock of where you are in relation to your target and discuss what might be done at that stage to boost the campaign.

My advice is simple: be nice, be professional, but be insistent they resolve problems immediately. If you succeed, they will claim it was the brilliance of their service. If you fail it will be (according to them) because you didn't do enough to make the campaign a success.

Keep feeding positive news!

Positive news about your business successes during the campaign works wonders.

You must conjure up a reason to stay in touch with your prospective investors. We touched on this already, but the key here is to make your investor feel they have made a good decision. And for those not yet committed, it's to gently push them over the edge to pledge.

Good news can take many forms:

— We just signed an important new customer

— Peter White has agreed to join us as Chief Financial Officer

— We've hit our revenue target for March

— Our KPIs on customer acquisition costs show we're 10 per cent better than target in Q1

— Jo Bloggs has just pledged £25,000 and wanted us to share that news

— We've just passed 50 per cent of our target in only 25 per cent of the campaign length

Am I getting noticed? Deploying and tracking the media campaign

The cheapest way to track anything at the time of writing is Google Alerts. Search for Google Alerts within your browser and follow the set-up process. Set up as many keywords as you like, and every time that word (or expression) is mentioned online, anywhere in the world, you'll get an email to tell you about it with the link.

You can use this to see when your name or the name of your company is mentioned. But you can also follow your competitors, or any other events that might affect your company.

Proactively answering questions from potential investors

Earlier in the chapter, I set out the process by which queries raised by your investors can be answered and shared with other investors. That's being reactive.

But you can also be proactive. It's not fraudulent to make up questions and answer them yourself. In fact, before the campaign starts it's a good idea to create a FAQ document. You don't release it, but it's on hand with pre-prepared answers that you and your team can use to get the responses right and be consistent. It also means you're all 'on message'. This means that you could say to your potential investor base:

A question you may be asking yourself is what we intend to use the new funds for? Here's what we hope will be a helpful answer . . .

Typical questions might be:

— What is XYZ?

— Who owns XYZ?

— Who is employed by XYZ?

— When was the company formed?

— What does XYZ do?

— How big is the market for XYZ services?

— What is unique about XYZ's services?

— Who are XYZ's competition?

— Does XYZ have customers?

— What is the monthly revenue of XYZ?

— Does XYZ make a profit? If not, when is that expected?

— How much is XYZ raising in this round?

— What will XYZ do with the money?

— What is the deal being offered to investors?

— Who has already committed to invest?

— What will XYZ do if they don't raise all the funds?

You get the idea. Sit round a table with your colleagues and imagine all the most challenging questions you might ever be asked and write down (and learn!) the best, most convincing answer.

What to do if the campaign is flagging

The simple answer is, move to plan B! It may be trite, but you should always have a plan B, or a recovery plan.

Here are some possibilities:

- Get the crowdfunding company to grant you an extension and then up your efforts to get your contacts to invest, so as to revive the campaign momentum as it's perceived by the crowdfunding company's own crowd.

- You can improve the offer mid-campaign. The improved offer will have to apply to all investors – even those already pledged on the original terms

- Redouble your efforts. Can everyone really say they've busted a gut to do everything you asked of them? Have you all been sending out regular messages on social media and following up on all the leads that came in from your contacts?

8:

HITTING (OR MISSING) YOUR TARGET

We've reached our target – what to do next?

One last little hurdle.

When your campaign target is reached, or more probably exceeded, there is a cooling-off period for the investors of 2 weeks. During that time, they can change their mind – even if they have given consent for money to be taken from their account when the campaign reaches its target. You won't have a chance to discuss their decision – or even know which investors have backed out.

So what could happen is that you slip back below 100 per cent of target. But provided you slip back to no more than 90 per cent of your target, the crowdfunding company is permitted to declare your campaign a success and draw funds down from the investors.

Getting the money into your bank account ASAP

Once the money is fully received from all investors, the crowdfunding company will transfer funds into your account, around 7 working days after the campaign is deemed 'closed'.

You will then receive a full list of all the investors, their individual investment amounts, and their contact details.

At this stage, your contract with the crowdfunding company is terminated and you have no further obligations to them nor they to you, other than continuing restrictions on confidentiality.

How to say thank you

You'll now have all your investors' contact details. There will be essential practical communications to make to them going forward, but for now, saying thank you is a wise action on the path to good investor relations.

My recommendation is to do it 'on brand', as they say. If you're a soup company, have some delivered to them or give them a voucher to buy your product. You can also simply pick up the phone and say thank you personally. I've held a drinks party before to good effect. Getting your investors 'engaged' is very beneficial; you'll find they act as unpaid ambassadors for your business, service or product – which reduces your customer acquisition costs. And for them, it's fun. They will want to meet fellow investors and many will want to stay close to you as the company progresses. They will also be inclined to provide useful feedback and practical help if they feel their assistance or know-how is welcome.

Delivering your short-term promises
– aka dishing out those rewards

Don't allow too large a time gap between campaign closure and delivery of the rewards. Your investors or donors will feel cheated if they have to chase you. And be sure to manage their expectations. If the printing of a book or T-shirt or organizing a dinner or lunch is going to take time, then let them know a likely date of delivery. And then stick to it!

Staying in touch – opening a channel for
regular communications with your donors
or investors

The simplest way nowadays is via email or other electronic media. But here are my suggested points of contact going forward:

— 'Thank you' communication

— Distribution of shareholders' list with shares held (but not amounts invested)

— Invitation to initially engage – either a call or at an event

— Quarterly shareholders' update – brief summary of trading performance and financials

— Distribution of annual results summary

— Interim updates and communications with significant news

— Distribution of EIS certificates and other legal documents required by shareholders

— Regular offers relating to the product – or incentives to suggest reference sells

What to do if the campaign fails to hit the target

Topping up the funding yourself – a realistic plan?

One of the rules set out by the FCA is that you can't invest twice in the same campaign. Their reason is to prevent investors 'gaming' the system. If one of your pre-committed investors had, for example, £20,000 to invest, your strategy might be to get them to invest £10,000 at first to add to the campaign momentum, but then 'drip' two further tranches of £5,000 into the campaign when you felt it needed a bit of a lift. Not unreasonably, the FCA believe that this would create the illusion that three investors were involved and that more and more investors were supporting the plan, when the exact opposite would be true; that investor interest was waning and the same investor was bolstering the campaign.

If, after all your efforts, the campaign fails to reach the target in the time given then I'm afraid that's it – but for one last opportunity.

And that is this. Crowdfunding companies are not permitted to give you the names of the investors who pledged funds towards your campaign . . . unless you have engaged with them *during* the campaign. For example, if a potential investor uses the crowdfunding company's bulletin board, where they can ask you questions, then you will know who they are and will have been given their contact details.

So, using the email addresses you've gathered from the crowdfunding campaign, you can subsequently go back to them and seek their investment or funding support outside of that campaign. When you add together these new contacts to your original committed investors (from the pre-campaign), you may find you're not far short of your target. Make this happen quickly at the end of the campaign – those that you engaged with will still be enthusiastic. Leave it too long and they will assume the opportunity to invest has gone.

Clearly, if your target was £100,000 and you only get a total of £35,000 commitment, that strategy isn't going to work. But if you were at £80,000, then I'd go back to all the investors and tell them that if they each put in 25 per cent more you'd hit target.

If they won't invest more, then go back to your financial plan and see if you can legitimately reduce the amount you're asking for. It could be that you and your colleagues are prepared to accept lower salaries in the early stages, or that during the campaign you've closed a good bit of business which is creating some unexpected but welcome additional cash, or that someone has offered you some office space. In all cases, you'll be able to reduce the cash required in the plan.

One final positive point. These restrictions on 'topping up' from the FCA don't apply to rewards campaigns – the occasions where no equity is being sold in your company. In that case you can freely top up the campaign yourself, close out, and call it a success!

Retiring gracefully – how to walk away while keeping everyone happy

Even if your campaign has 'failed', you still have an asset – you have a list of investors that trust you to run a business, and are willing to back you. Get in contact with them all and thank them. Tell them your plan. Ask for any ideas. Regard them as your best buddies from now on. Your next project (assuming you drop this one) may be more successful at attracting funds, and those investors will give you a massive head start.

Thank the crowdfunding company too. If you feel they've done their best for you, then you might want to use them again. Don't expect huge post-campaign support from them if you've missed target – remember they've invested time in you and gained nothing, so they'll want to minimize any extra effort. But the better ones will help you understand what could have been done more effectively, or explain the context in which your campaign was run. It could be that a major event like Brexit caused otherwise enthusiastic investors to hold back, or that you were up against stiff competition for attention and funds – not just on the same crowdfunding platform but also across all the others.

Learning from what went wrong

Although crowdfunding companies will be disinclined to over-analyse why your campaign failed, that's not to say you can't press them for their view. You might ask for the following:

— What is the main reason we failed?

— Were we clear enough about why what we do is unique?

— Was our offer sufficiently compelling – i.e. not overpriced?

— Did our management look credible enough?

— Did we handle the questions OK?

— What external factors might have held our campaign back?

— Were our presentation materials (video, spreadsheets, data, research) sufficiently professional?

Picking yourself up

OK, let's move to Plan B. In a fascinating 2014 article entitled 'Study Shows Business is Better the Second Time Around', Scott Volpe quotes from Allison Schrager research. It found that Texan retailers were less successful than the national average for small businesses: one in four closed after a year; half after two.

What happened next, she says, was telling. Of the first-time entrepreneurs whose businesses closed quickly, the overwhelming majority, 71 per cent, didn't bother to try again. But the tenacious 29 per cent who did were more likely to be successful the second, third and even tenth time around.

Somewhat paradoxically, their success rate increased with their number of past failures.

The researchers argue that experience, even when it's not positive, is invaluable – that entrepreneurs learn effectively from mistakes as well as from successes. They even found that serial entrepreneurs are successful in new types of businesses. Experience owning a hair salon translates into more success at running a clothing store. (There's one important exception: first-time restaurant owners, no matter their business background, tend to fail; serial restaurateurs are more successful.)[9]

So, assuming you've not tried and failed three times already, you should put this campaign failure behind you.

Tell yourself:

- A failed crowdfunding campaign is NOT a vote of no confidence in your business – it's just that your great idea didn't match the interests at that time of those specific investors.

- Perseverance is at the core of every successful person. So, you're not going to give up, are you?

- There are always other ways to fund a company – one of which is to try another crowdfunding campaign! Nothing is stopping you, and rival crowdfunding companies may be keen to show they can deliver you investors where their rival failed.

- It's smart to review everything. If you've failed because a weak member of the team created a negative impression among investors, then part company. Review every aspect of the campaign and see where you can tighten up where you fell short.

- Lastly, consider mothballing your project for a while – you may find that something happens in the market that turns your idea into something very topical. Your home energy-saving device, for example, could suddenly become hot property if gas or electricity prices took a jump.

9:

CONCLUSION: SECRETS OF SUCCESS

Making regular fundraising part of growing your business

Back in chapter 4 I cautioned you to neither over- nor underfund your company. Don't raise so little that, if sales are harder to come by or costs loom larger, you run out of cash. Neither should you give away too much equity when the company's not worth much, especially when you don't really need all the cash at that time.

The challenge is to ride the optimum 'cusp' between funding and selling equity.

The keys to success in this matter are milestones and traction. As your business is growing, you'll want to set points in your progress at which future success is more assured. At these points risk is reduced, and therefore the likelihood of investors achieving their investment return is increased. Investors will pay more for a company that is showing success. Here are some examples of milestones:

- You're cash break-even, meaning your revenue has reached the point where you're covering your costs on a monthly basis. This tells the investor that the risk of failure, while still in the background, is greatly reduced, and, as such, you're all upside from now on. Your value has increased.

- The point at which there is a clear relationship between the cost of winning a customer and the lifetime value of that customer. If you know that to win a subscriber costs £150, and they are proven to subscribe – on average – for 25 months at £30 per month, on which you make £10 profit, then you know each £150 investment will generate £250 of profit. That means that, if the market is scalable, you could raise £1.5m to invest in marketing and you know it will yield £2.5m profit, which could make your company 5 × £2.5m, so £12.5m more valuable. A good investment return. (The '5' here is the multiple of profits typical for your industry sector.)

- You've landed a major customer who will give you regular, stable revenue that will increase over time. Big-name endorsements for your product give investor confidence and suggest you'll now be able to attract other customers of a similar scale.

- You've hired an impressive executive. While this alone would be insufficient to go back to the market to raise more funds, it indicates that you're impressive enough to attract top talent.

- Overall, the most compelling reason to raise capital is when you have a valid reason to spend the money. And this could be a new product, an opportunity to open-up your business in another country, or perhaps even make an acquisition.

The trick is to make the right call at the right time to

raise capital. And, if you can, to devote less and less time as the entrepreneur to securing each round of new investment.

Once you've done one round of crowdfunding you may not need to do another. Your next round could be with a trade investor (a strategic partner), or a venture capital firm. But however you raise funds, you will want the process to be quick, cheap and efficient with your executives' time.

One route open to you is to issue an option or warrant at the time of your next funding round. This is a route to making that next round very quick and easy. Providing, of course, your business has grown in line with or in excess of your forecasts! Say you issue 1 option for every 3 shares during your fundraising equity round. If an investor has bought £60,000's worth of shares they will have the right, or option, to buy a further £20,000's worth at a future date (say 18 months ahead) and at, usually, a higher share price or 'the option price'. If the shares are worth more in 18 months than the option price, the investor will usually agree to 'exercise' the option and so purchase more shares. And so you will have secured further funding from most of your investors at that future date. Easy!

There are almost no companies that haven't wanted to or needed to raise successive rounds of funding. Very often it's for benign reasons – like the need for more working capital, or to accelerate growth. Build this approach into your master plan. That way you'll plan better, and not get taken by surprise with a funding need, which might leave you with too little time to pull it off on your terms.

Some final tips

There's so much advice I can give you to increase the chances of your company being a success, but perhaps that's for another book.

So as not to leave you empty-handed, here's my general advice.

- Now you've raised the funds, spend them! Companies have to deliver on their plans. You can go bust just as easily by not making spending decisions – like not doing the marketing you need, or not hiring key staff – as you can from overspending on operating costs.

- Winkle out weak members of your team. Especially if they have a large stake in the business. It will only cause heartache and trouble later – not to mention litigation – if you let the problem fester.

- Don't give away equity too cheaply. You may be tempted to 'gift' equity or grant a generous number of options in lieu of salary. Hats off to you for thinking this way – it's smart cash conservancy. If your business will be worth £10m in five years' time, and let's say that one of your top executives will be paid on average £80,000 p.a. over that period, then they will earn £400,000 in total. Then I would double that to £800,000 with shares. So, their shares should be worth £400,000 when you sell. That's 4 per cent of the equity (i.e. 400,000 / 10,000,000). Not the 10 per cent or 15 per cent they may demand.

- Get a great lawyer and get them to draft a good shareholders' agreement – one that ensures you have the freedom to get on with running the business without constant shareholder approval.

- Surround yourself with a strong board. Don't pay them in cash if you can get their agreement. If they are worth £15,000 p.a. in fees (which you want to pay as shares), then use my 'double up' approach and offer them £15,000's worth of shares in total. Allocate them as an option with an exercise price the same as the company's share price at the time of grant and have them 'rest' over 4 years.

- Be cautious when choosing a chairman. The role carries more power than you may realize. If they turn against you, it's trouble. Choose someone you totally trust, and don't go for the great and good. They can be pompous and presume all they need to do is turn up for board meetings. Go for someone who knows your sector and who has built a company of your scale before, and has done so relatively recently.

- Keep your board as small as you can. You must always control the board in voting numbers. Don't find yourself as the only executive among a larger number of non-execs.

- A good finance director is the backbone of success. Always. They don't need to be full-time at first

- Don't underestimate the importance of building for scale, particularly in terms of accounting, management reporting and corporate governance.

It may seem like overkill to produce a management report with supporting financials each month – especially if your initial board is informal. But do it. Set a pattern and it will serve you well all the way up to being a significant scale company. After all, you need good control feedback to manage the business, don't you?

- Track everything. If it moves, track it as a KPI (key performance indicator). And chart all the stats – it's the only way to spot trends.

- Sales, sales, sales! Make winning sales and creating revenue your number one priority. You can always control costs – that's easy. And be flexible. If your master plan for winning customers at the fundraising stage isn't working then pivot quickly.

- But don't worry about your competition too much. Talk to your customers all the time and let them drive your innovation and customer experience. You'll then naturally stay ahead, because you will provide the services that your customers most want.

- Employ cleverer people than you. As an entrepreneur, your most important skills are passion and judgement. You need to have a relentless determination and to make more good decisions than bad ones. Know-how is cheap, and experience a little more expensive. Just hire them – they are a commodity.

- Be a benign dictator! Be collegiate in the way you listen to the opinions and advice of your colleagues and your board, but make your own decisions. Don't go with the majority if you have a counterview. The buck stops with you, so you alone have to make the decisions. You'll probably be the only one with a true broad perspective on all facets of the business and your market. Your judgement is the one that matters most.

- Build a brand. Work out the true personality and proposition of your company and ensure it pervades throughout your company as it grows. If you can make your culture fun and stimulating then your customers will love you, the competition will be disheartened, you'll attract the staff you want and won't lose the staff you care about.

- Take care of home life. You're going to need an understanding partner. Involve them in the good things, like successes, not just your worries. Put in long hours but counterbalance that with planned rewards, like weekends away or things to look forward to.

- Think of the planet and society at large. Be socially responsible, ethical, open and honest in the way you deal with everyone. But make no mistake: you can do more good by creating a successful, sustainable, profitable, tax-paying company that creates ever growing employment, than you can worrying about purchasing recycled paper.

- Remember – you are the elite, and one of a rare group of individuals that create change and progression in economies and society. Every major corporation was a start-up at some point. Think big. Be proud. Have fun!

FURTHER READING

Legal issues – compliance with Financial Conduct Authority (FCA) rules

Crowdfunding falls within the Financial Conduct Authority's scope of regulation. The FCA limits the type of person that crowdfunding platforms can send direct-offer financial promotions to.

Investors must fall into one of the following categories:

— Certified or self-certified sophisticated investors

— Certified high net worth investors

— A person who confirms they will receive regulated investment advice or investment management services from an authorized person before any financial promotion is made to them

— A person who certifies they will not invest more than 10 per cent of their net investible portfolio in unlisted shares or unlisted debt securities

Ensure that the crowdfunding website you use is authorized and regulated by the FCA. You can search the FCA register at https://register.fca.org.uk.

Tax issues – sorting out the tax breaks for your investors

Investors will want to know if tax relief is available. The most common forms of tax relief are SEIS (Seed Enterprise Investment Scheme) and EIS (Enterprise Investment Scheme).

Each scheme provides differing degrees of income tax relief and capital gains tax relief, for which more detail can be found at:

https://www.gov.uk/guidance/seed-enterprise-investment-scheme-background#capital-gains-tax-reinvestment-relief

and:

https://www.gov.uk/government/publications/the-enterprise-investment-scheme-introduction/enterprise-investment-scheme

The company, the shares being issued and the investor have to meet certain criteria in order for the reliefs to be obtained. The company will need to maintain its status for the relevant qualifying period, which may be at odds with the commercial needs of the company in the future. The company should ensure that it does not give any binding commitment to maintain its qualifying status for SEIS or EIS.

Investors will usually expect the company to have obtained advanced assurance from HMRC in respect of SEIS relief and/or EIS relief being available. There is more information on both schemes in Appendix IV.

Corporate issues – dealing with shareholder rights

Shareholder rights are normally governed by the articles of association of the company and, in certain circumstances, a shareholders' agreement.

The articles of association bind all shareholders and the company and are available for inspection at Companies House. A shareholders' agreement is a private document which binds only those persons who are party to it.

Most crowdfunding sites will seek to avoid the added complication of a shareholders' agreement and will try and deal with all shareholder rights in the articles of association. Typical matters that are dealt with are:

— Who can appoint directors

— Matters which require specific levels of consent from shareholders

— Pre-emption rights on new issues of shares

— Pre-emption rights on transfers of shares

— Permitted share transfers

— Matters governing exits e.g. drag-along and tag-along rights

— Good leaver/bad leaver provisions

— Governance issues – adhering to company law and contractual obligations

Subject to any matters specifically reserved for shareholder consent in the articles or shareholders' agreement, day-to-day management of the company is reserved for the board of directors.

Companies should:

— Establish a regular pattern of board meetings that is suitable for the company e.g. once a month, once a quarter

— Establish clear delegation of authority to individual directors where applicable

— Ensure filing requirements with Companies House are understood and complied with

In respect of contracts companies should:

— Ensure that contracts are documented, signed and stored in an easily accessible manner

— Understand the essential terms of the contract, such as payment term, termination conditions, and liability

— Conduct regular reviews of contracts to ensure renewal and termination deadlines are not missed

Other issues:

— Where applicable, register with the Information Commissioner for a data protection registration

— Consider any other licences or consents that may be required for the conduct of business, e.g. consumer credit act licences

— Ensure intellectual property rights are properly secured and registered where necessary

— Ensure all employees have written contracts of employment

— Be aware of pension regulation and auto enrolment – see http://www.thepensionsregulator.gov.uk/en/employers

APPENDIX I

SETTING UP A COMPANY

In line with the government's 2016 Small Business, Enterprise and Employment Act update, the information you require to form a private company limited by shares (the most popular company structure in the UK) has changed. Here's a list of the information you'll need to provide to Companies House, or a formation agent, when you start a company.

The following will be on the public register, unless otherwise stated:

1. Unique company name

Companies House can let you know immediately if your name is available. See https://beta.companieshouse.gov.uk. And don't forget to check with startups.co.uk, where you can get guidance on choosing a company name via this URL: http://startups.co.uk/can-i-call-my-company-whatever-i-like/.

2. Registered office

This is the official address for the company and must be based in the UK. However, the company need not trade from or even have anyone based at the address, as long as government mail is forwarded onto the company directors.

3. Director name(s)

The person or people tasked with running the company are its directors. A company must have at least one person acting as the director. The following information is needed when appointing a director:

— Name
— Date of birth (the month and year is on the public register; the day is not)
— Nationality
— Occupation
— Country of residence
— Service address (similar to the registered office, this is the director's 'official' address)

Their residential address is not on the public register, unless the address is also being used as the service address.

Corporate directors

While a company can't be a director of itself, another company can be appointed as a director (as long as at least one person has been appointed too). The following is required when appointing a corporate director:

— Company name
— Authorizing person's name

— Address

— EEA/Non-EEA

— Country registered

— Registration number

— Governing law

— Legal form

4. Shareholder name(s)

The person or people who own the company are its share-holders. A company limited by shares can be formed with one person acting as both the director and the shareholder. To appoint a shareholder you will need their:

— Name

— Address

— Allotment of shares

You can read more about setting up a limited company at www.companiesmadesimple.com.

Corporate shareholders

A company can't be a shareholder of itself, but another company can be a shareholder. When appointing a corporate shareholder you will need the:

— Company name

— Authorizing person's name

— Address

— Allotment of shares

5. Standard Industry Classification (SIC) code

A SIC code is a five-digit number that outlines the industry that the company will be working in.[10] Not sure what industry you'll be working in yet? Simply use the code 82990 (other business support service activities). You can update this code when filing a confirmation statement.

6. People with significant control

This has been introduced as part of the Small Business, Enterprise and Employment Act 2015. The aim is to increase transparency in businesses by showing who really owns and runs a company. According to the government, a person with significant control is anyone who:

— owns more than 25 per cent of the company's shares

— holds more than 25 per cent of the company's voting rights

— holds the right to appoint or remove the majority of directors

— has the right to, or actually exercises, significant influence or control

— holds the right to exercise, or actually exercises, significant control over a trust or company that meets one of the first four conditions.

For each person with significant control you will need to document their name, date of birth, nationality, occupation, country of residence and service address (their residential address is not on the public register unless the address is also being used as the service address). You will also need to document the nature of control.

Company secretary

This is now an optional appointment. Traditionally, the role was taken by the person who would be responsible for various admin tasks. If you do decide to appoint a secretary you will need to document their name and their service address.

7. Memorandum and articles

This is the set of documents that outline how your company will be run. If you decide to form your company with a formation agent, they can provide you with memorandum and articles that suit the majority of companies.

And there you have it, all the information you need to form a private company limited by shares.

Appendix II

CHOOSING A DOMAIN NAME

Top 10 tips on how to choose a domain name

One decision that you'll have to live with for quite a long time is the domain name you choose for your site. You may have a list of options that you know are available, but what should you keep in mind when you sit down to make the decision?

If you're setting up a new company the chances are that you're starting a new brand, but you may already have a name and identity for your new organization and now need an appropriate domain name to go with it.

The brand name you choose is critical of course, but so is the domain name for your company or brand's online presence. The following guidelines should help you when making your choice.

1. Keep it 'brandable'

This means the name you choose should sound like a brand, and not a generic term. 'pastapronto' instead of 'quickcook-pasta'. Always avoid hyphens and numbers, as they rarely sound or look like a brand.

To continue with the pasta theme, if your company is a pasta recipe website that also sells pasta-related products, then the obvious choice might be pasta-shop.com – but that would be hard to register, might already be taken and doesn't lend itself well to being branded.

Generic names can be both hard to remember and difficult to make stand out, plus, in the long term, your competitors will devise Google AdWords phrases that copy your generic expressions (which they're allowed to do provided the words are generic) and you'll lose marketing effectiveness.

Domain names that might work for you are:

— pastamagic.com

— pastalavista.com

— pastayourway.com

— pastarecipesonline.com

Pastarecipesonline.com is still pretty generic, but pastamagic.com might work well because the brand identity lends itself to the use of a memorable visual reference to magic.

2. Make it easy to say

Making your domain name easy to pronounce is really important, because it will make it more memorable. Take these three examples:

— thepizzarecipecompany.com

— flourpower.com

— eggznflour.com

Arguably the best domain name here is thepizzarecipecompany.com, because it is memorable and there's no ambiguity about the spelling. Someone remembering the name flourpower.com would almost certainly type in the spelling 'flower', and a wise competitor could register flower-power.com and link to their company, which may have a completely different domain, such as yummypizza.com. Same goes for eggznflour. Easy to remember the name, but almost impossible to search for it correctly.

3. Make it short

The best domain names are usually as short as they can be without compromising on points 1 and 2 above. Long domain names may need to be abbreviated on social media or might not show fully in links, which isn't ideal. Take these three examples:

— pastaheaven.com
— pastaweekend.com
— pastascience.com

All of these are a similar length, but beware of choosing something that can be shortened by others. For example, pastaweekend.com might get listed in directories as pastawe.com, while pastascience.com could get shortened to pastasci.com, which loses memorability and impact. In these examples, pastaheaven.com is the best choice.

4. Make '.com' your first choice

Almost every word in every language, and every expression or saying, is pretty much taken now as a domain with a '.com' suffix. But it's still the most internationally recognized suffix to use, and it's still the one all companies try to get. You may have to pay a premium for it to the canny company or individual that registered it ahead of you, but think of this as a start-up, once-only cost and go for the best domain. It will add value to the company if you eventually sell the business.

There's also an argument that domains ending in .eu or .biz or .tv are simply not in the mindset of the humble consumer. They will, whoever they are, know about .com.

The .com suffix might not be the best bet if you expressly want to associate your business with a location – such as the UK. It's for that reason that the BBC has chosen www.bbc. co.uk, even though it owns the .com. Try it yourself – search for bbc.com and you'll be routed to the .co.uk website. In our example, therefore, pastamagic.co.uk would be a good name. And this would be the best name available to you if the .com is already taken. But beware, the owner of pasta-magic.com may start to trade in your territory and will mop up all the Google search traffic you were enjoying until they came along.

5. Avoid the risk of infringement

It's crucial to avoid domain names that could be confused with another company's existing trademark. You run the risk of being prosecuted for infringement. Do your research carefully and take legal advice about this if you have any concerns. These potential problems do happen regularly and have done throughout the history of the internet, where a trademark owner will sue a domain owner, even if that owner is using the domain legitimately for business purposes. If in doubt – avoid!

6. Associate the domain name with what you do

Ideally your domain name will immediately conjure up an image of what your company does in the mind of the potential customer or supporter. recipemagic.com or pasta-perfected.com work in this way, whereas something like zippomania.com might leave your customers baffled.

Your challenge is to choose something helpfully descriptive and yet not generic. The Pizza Express restaurant chain brand, like the Vithit vitamin drink company brand, say what they do. But, again by way of argument, you can choose an unrelated name provided you have the marketing funds to make your domain and company name inextricably associated with what you do. So, Esso was able to rebrand part of its operations into Exxon because of the enormity of the marketing funds it could commit to embedding the new name in petrol buyers' minds and memory. My general advice is to combine something factually associated with what you do with a positive word, adjective or attribute that will lift the name and leave a positive impression. Examples:

— pastaperfection.com

— readyrecipes.com

— pleasingpasta.com

7. Be careful when using keywords in the name

You may think that using keywords in your domain name would aid Google organic placing (how high up the page your domain name is listed). But Google are wise to this and their algorithms discount domain name keywords, to a certain extent. There is a fine line to tread between choosing a memorable name that indicates what your website is all about and stringing together keywords for good SEO (Search Engine Optimization) – if it's too 'good' it will backfire. Take these potential domain names, for example:

— recipesforpasta.com

— buypastaonline.com

— freshpastarecipes.com

— pastamagic.com

Recipesforpasta.com and buypastaonline.com are ones to avoid for the reasons above. freshpastarecipes.com has keywords, but also 'fresh', so will be a better option than the first two suggestions, and pastamagic.com will rise up the search rankings with good SEO planning. SEO is driven by good content on your website and the associated backlinks from magazines, bloggers and other media. If you think about a brand website like Amazon.com, which clearly has no association with what it is, or Google itself, or a domain here in the UK like bbc.co.uk, these are very, very well branded and associated with their niches, but they don't have keyword richness.

8. Be creative with the name

If your domain name is not available, it is fine to add a suffix or a prefix (but remember point 5 above regarding infringement). It's OK to use an alternate extension and be creative.

— thepastarecipecompany.com

— thefreshpastacompany.com

— freshpastaonline.com

— pastamagicrecipes.com

All these examples work if you've already got a business or a project that includes the name offline. You may already have a small pasta supply business that distributes through wholesale channels, but you've now decided to crowdfund some additional capital and take the company online, selling directly to the consumer. In that example adding words like 'the' or 'company' won't detract from the core memorability of your domain.

9. Avoid numbers and punctuation

There are a few examples of successfully mixing letters with numbers, but they are rare and they have almost certainly been associated with companies that have thrown significant marketing budgets at promoting the brand.

The reason to avoid this is simply that if you're adding a hyphen or full stop to your chosen domain, then chances are there's already a conventionally written .com in existence and you will run into infringement problems, or at the very least find that the owner of the better, simpler name will take the bulk of the Google search traffic away from you.

Here are some examples of what not to do – even if the .com domain is available:

— pasta.recipes.com

— magic-pasta.com

— flour+eggs+water.com

— pasta4all.com

10. The domain as an asset

Many years ago, I became the chairman of a company that had the name Logotron, and traded with the domain logotron.co.uk.

Hidden in the cupboard, as it were, was the domain name logo.com, which didn't fully fit with the company's trading brand. We eventually put it into auction in New York (where these things are best traded) and we grossed, before commission, $500,000. That enabled us to push forward plans very quickly, without the need for a funding round.

The moral of the story is that a great domain name is still worth a lot of money to the right company. If you can find a name that works for your company, there is the potential of adding to the shareholder value of the company way beyond conventional valuation based on its financial or trading performance!

Appendix III

USING THE BRAND PYRAMID TO DEFINE YOUR BRAND

This section has been written by Lucian Camp, Principal, Lucian Camp Consulting[11]

Like most marketing terms and ideas, the meaning of the word 'brand' and the process you go through to define what it means for your own business are a little fuzzy.

But most people would agree on the key points. As for what a brand is, you wouldn't hear much disagreement if you said that your brand is the sum total of the perceptions of your business and your product or service that exist in the minds of your target audience. Or, more concisely, it's everything that people think, feel and know about you.

You'd see most experts nodding their heads if you said that the process of building a brand starts with a clear, succinct definition of the perceptions you wish to build. This requires some kind of workshop process, to debate, discuss and agree what those perceptions should be. And that, in turn, requires the use of a tool or template, to provide structure and focus to that workshop.

That's where a bit of the fuzziness creeps in, because there are any number of tools or templates available. Some experts swear by the 'brand onion' (yes, seriously). Others prefer the 'brand prism'. I've come across the brand kernel and the brand narrative. Brand stories are very popular at the moment.

However, when I'm running brand-definition workshops, I favour what I think is the simplest and clearest tool, the tried and tested Brand Pyramid.

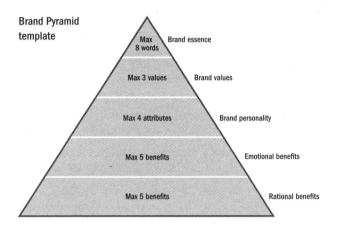

Brand Pyramid template

- Max 8 words — Brand essence
- Max 3 values — Brand values
- Max 4 attributes — Brand personality
- Max 5 benefits — Emotional benefits
- Max 5 benefits — Rational benefits

As you can see from this template, the pyramid aims to define the main points of the brand perceptions you're aiming to build on five levels. Working from the bottom up, these are:

Rational Benefits: In measurable, left-brain terms, what are the key benefits that we wish to be seen to offer?

Emotional Benefits: In qualitative, right-brain terms, how do we want people to feel good about what we have to offer?

Brand Personality: In ordinary, human terms, how do we come across to people? Are we warm and friendly? Cool and professional? Dynamic and exciting?

Brand Values: What are the values that distinguish the way we do business? Do we have an unbreakable commitment to, say, keeping things simple? Or being innovative and breaking new ground? Or putting our customers' interests first? Or . . . what, exactly?

Brand Essence: As succinctly and clearly as possible, what is it that we're here to do for our customers? How do we sum up our promise to them?

You'll also notice notes on the pyramid template, rationing the number of separate ideas which you should include in it. There's no science to this, and many brand experts wouldn't recognize these numbers – but in my experience, these limits help to keep the finished product clear and focused.

You may wonder how this brand pyramid approach connects with Julian Costley's approach in chapter 5, where he says that 'Brand = Personality + Promise'. I think it connects very strongly. The two 'benefits' levels express the promise; the personality and the values levels together express the personality; and it all comes together in the essence, at the very top.

So how do we make the journey from empty template to completed and agreed brand pyramid? Through a simple workshop structure – in my working life, hardly a week goes by without my moderating at least one of these. In outline, the process goes like this:

1. **Decide who you want to attend.** Any number between three and eight people is good. All should have some sense of a) what the business is about, and b) the market you're targeting.

2. **Pull together and circulate relevant available insight.** This could be anything from research findings among your target market, to a review of what your competitors are saying and doing.

3. **Set aside at least half a day.**

4. **Tackle the pyramid from the bottom up.**

5. **For each level, start by brainstorming all the possible ideas everyone can think of.** Capture everything on a whiteboard or flipchart. When you can't think of any more, discuss and debate the shortlist (no more than the number that appears on the template). Shortlisted ideas should ideally be those which: are important to our target market and are distinctive to your business.

   However, when push comes to shove, being important to the target market matters more. There is no value in ideas which are distinctive to your business if you don't think your market cares about them.

6. **Work your way up all five levels, longlisting and shortlisting as you go.** And obviously keeping the outputs from each level.

7. **Take away the sheets capturing the outputs, and draw up the initial brand pyramid.** This is a time-consuming task, best done by your moderator, if you have one.

8. **Review this first draft.** Do you buy it? Does it sound like your business, product or service? Does it

hang together and tell a story? Is it different? Most important of all, will it appeal to your market? Keep refining until you have positive answers to all these questions.

9. **Review with the workshop participants.** Once everyone is happy with the Brand Pyramid, you've completed this stage of the brand development process – you have the definition of the brand you're intending to build.

There is then the trifling matter of actually building it. What this entails will vary enormously depending on the nature of your business, product or service, the brand definition you have created and the nature of your target market. Essentially, though, it means taking every possible opportunity to project elements of your brand definition to your market. Note those key words: 'every possible opportunity'. This is emphatically not just about your name and logo, strapline and marketing communications.

On the contrary, it's about everything that touches your customer. If, say, you want to be seen to be clear and transparent, then that doesn't just mean having a website written in short sentences: it means having a pricing structure that is genuinely easy to understand too. If you want to be seen to be focused on your customers' needs, it doesn't just mean using the word 'you' a lot in your marketing copy: it means making sure your call centre answers their calls promptly, whenever customers need to talk to you. It doesn't take much to discredit your brand. Behave a few times in a way that contradicts the perceptions you're trying to establish, and you give yourself a mountain to climb.

And finally . . .

Keep your brand definition, and the progress you're making towards building the perceptions you want, under regular review. Research among customers and prospects has a vital role to play. Are there gaps in the perceptions you're creating? Do you need to increase your efforts in particular areas? Is the story you're telling as powerful as you had hoped? What are your competitors doing? Is there anything you're doing that's conflicting with your intentions, and if so, can you stop doing it?

Managing a brand is a dynamic, ongoing process, not a one-off at a single moment in time. But do it consistently and well, and you'll be adding value to what will almost certainly become your business's single most valuable asset.

Appendix IV
EIS AND SEIS

This section has been written by the team at Crowdcube, www.crowdcube.com

Enterprise Investment Scheme (EIS) overview

The Enterprise Investment Scheme is designed to help smaller, higher-risk companies raise finance by offering tax relief on new shares in those companies that qualify. For the investor, it's a tax-efficient way to invest in small companies – up to £1,000,000 per person per year in qualifying companies.

What makes it even more attractive is the 'carry back' facility, where investments can be applied to the preceding tax year.

Michael Portillo, Chief Secretary to the Treasury when the scheme was launched in 1993, said: 'The purpose of Enterprise Investment Schemes is to recognize that unquoted trading companies can often face considerable difficulties in realizing relatively small amounts of share capital. The new scheme is intended to provide a well-targeted means for some of those problems to be overcome.'

More than twenty years later, those 'considerable difficulties' in raising small amounts of capital are still a pertinent feature of the business landscape.

What tax reliefs are available?

1. Income Tax relief

There is no minimum investment through EIS in any one company in any one tax year. Tax relief of 30 per cent can be claimed on investments (up to £1,000,000 in one tax year) giving a maximum tax reduction in any one year of £300,000, provided you have sufficient income tax liability to cover it.

EIS allowances are allocated individually; therefore, a married couple could invest up to £2 million each tax year and be eligible for income tax relief. The shares must be held for at least three years from the date of issue or the tax relief will be withdrawn.

People connected with the company are not eligible for income tax relief on their shares.

2. Capital Gains Tax (CGT) exemption

Any gain is CGT free if the shares are held for at least three years and the income tax relief was claimed on them. Shares can be held for much longer and therefore potentially enable the investor to accrue their CGT exemption over a long period of time, which can be a great attraction.

3. Loss relief

If shares are disposed of at a loss, the investor can elect that the amount of the loss, less income tax relief given, can be set against income of the year in which they were disposed, or on income of the previous year, instead of being set against any capital gains.

4. CGT deferral relief

Payment of CGT can be deferred when the gain is invested in shares of an EIS qualifying company. The gain can be made from the disposal of any kind of asset but the investment must be made one year before or three years after the gain arose – connection to company does not matter. Unconnected investors are eligible for relief from both income tax and CGT deferral.

Carry back

There is a 'carry back' facility, which allows all or part of the cost of shares acquired in one tax year to be treated as though those shares had been acquired in the preceding tax year. Relief is then given against the income tax liability of that preceding year, rather than against the tax year in which those shares were acquired. This is subject to the overriding limit for relief for each year.

For more information please see the HMRC website:

https://www.gov.uk/hmrc-internal-manuals/
venture-capital-schemes-manual/vcm10530

Restrictions

Connection to the company

Should the investor be connected to the company, they are not eligible for income tax relief. Connections are defined through financial interest or employment.

Connection by financial interest

An individual is connected with the company if they control the company or hold more than 30 per cent of the share capital or voting rights. These conditions apply for up to two years before and three years after the share issue. If, during this time, the individual becomes connected, then the relief will be withdrawn. All relatives except brothers and sisters are included within these restrictions.

Connection by employment

Partners, directors and employees of the company are all connected with it and therefore not eligible, as are associates. Associates are business partners, trustees and relatives. Again, these conditions apply for up to two years before and three years after the share issue.

The only exceptions are business angels – where the connection is as a director who receives no remuneration from the company.

Claiming your tax relief

The investor can only claim relief once the company sends through an EIS3 form. Claims are made through the self-assessment tax return for the tax year in which the shares were issued.

Claims can be made up to five years after the investment after the first 31 January following the tax year in which the investment was made.

Tax relief that is reduced or withdrawn

Tax relief will be withdrawn if you become connected to the company or if the company loses its qualifying status.

The relief will be either reduced or withdrawn if the shares are disposed of or if the investor receives 'value' from the company, such as a loan or an asset below market value.

Examples

Here are a few examples of how EIS tax relief works. To make the maths easy, let's assume you invest £10,000 in each case and you're in the 45 per cent tax bracket.

Case 1: The company does well and doubles its value and you hold the shares for three years

Investment = £10,000
Income Tax relief = £3,000 (as a reduction in your
    income tax bill)
Capital Gains Tax = £Zero
Your gain = £13,000 (£10,000 profit from the sale
    plus £3,000 income tax relief)

Case 2: The company value stays the same

Investment = £10,000
Income Tax relief = £3,000 (as a reduction in your
    income tax bill)
Share sales = £10,000
Your gain = £3,000 (from the income tax relief)

Case 3: The company closes and your shares are worth nothing

Investment = £10,000

Income Tax relief = £3,000 (as a reduction in your income tax bill)

At risk capital = £7,000

Loss relief on at risk capital @ 45 per cent = £3,150

Your actual loss = £3,850

(£10,000 – [£3,000 + £3,150])

Please note

The availability of any tax relief, including EIS and SEIS, depends on the individual circumstances of each investor and of the company concerned, and may be subject to change in the future. If you are in any doubt about the availability of any tax reliefs, or the tax treatment of your investment, you should obtain independent tax advice before proceeding with your investment.

Appendix V
TIPS ON SHAPING A BOARD

The minimum number of board members you need in a UK private company is one, and they don't need to be a shareholder.

My general advice when setting up a company is to be the director yourself, as you'll most likely be the one to set up the company bank account, and the bank will need a director to sign the application forms and give signatures in the mandate that dictates signing of cheques.

Even as the company grows, try and keep the size of the board as small as you can – it speeds up decision-making, gives you less people to persuade to follow your strategy and tactical decisions and reduces the number of people who can gang up against you if things start to go wrong.

But, as you grow and attract funds from friends and family, crowdfunding investors and angel investors, so the pressure will mount for them to have some representation around your board table. When that happens, try to appoint just one non-executive director who will act as the independent guardian of other shareholders' interests. In practice, if you've started a company with a colleague you'll want them on the board alongside the non-exec. And that means you'll have an ally when it comes to any board votes.

The most likely progression will be that, as you do successive rounds of financing, each representative of an investor group (such as a venture capital company) will want a seat on the board. Usually you won't have a choice if you want their money, as they'll make it a condition. But you can insist on having a veto on who's appointed. Here are a few guidelines on the ideal person you want on your board:

— They represent at least 10 per cent of the equity of your company – less and they shouldn't really be there

— You get on with them well and mutually respect each other's skills and experience

— They know your sector well and can add insight, advice and possibly mentoring

— They are accessible – meaning on the end of a phone if you need them, and close enough to be able to meet outside the fixed board dates for a quick chat over a coffee or lunch if you need their opinion

— They take the minimum fees, if any. Professional non-executive directors expect fees, but board directors who are there to represent their shareholding really shouldn't charge fees

— Check to make sure there are no conflicts of interest – that they're not a shareholder or on the board of your competition

Entrepreneurs often think they need to appoint a chair of the board. UK company law doesn't require a permanent chair role, but you will need to appoint one of the directors to chair the board meetings. This can be you. It's very old-fashioned now to appoint what I would call 'the great and the good' as your chair. These people are characterized by being close to retirement and tend to dine out on their (very often faded) market reputation. My advice, if you feel you need a figurehead in the company, is to pick someone who's freshly sold their business. They will still be 'hot' in the market and their involvement in your company will add gravitas.

What should you pay your directors? Executive directors are really your management, so that's whatever you've agreed with them for their full-time role. But a chair doing two or three days a month would expect perhaps £15,000 per annum at the start-up stage, rising to £25,000 once you're generating cash. A non-exec should get around £12,000, rising to £15,000.

How much of your equity should you give away? That's a tough question. My rule of thumb is equity to the same value as their fees. So, an incoming chair might get £15,000's worth of shares at the outset, most likely as options that vest over a four-year period. Same goes for the non-exec.

One of the questions I'm often asked by entrepreneurs is how often the board should meet and what should they be given in their pack of information. The simple answer is that you should meet at least monthly, and you should give them a subset of the information you need yourself to run the company. Never give a board information that you never use – if you don't value it, you can be sure they won't. Simple tip: Give them information, not data.

In summary, what makes a good board?

— A like-minded group of professionals who all want the company to succeed

- Full attendance by all directors, even if occasionally one or more are 'patched in' by conference call

- Short, fact-based meetings, with most of the information disseminated four working days before the meeting

- An effective chair who keeps to the agenda, makes sure all the important issues and decisions are dealt with and ensures everyone has an opportunity to contribute

- Well-written minutes that provide a clear actions list and form a definitive record of the board's decisions

- An absence of politics but a heap of humour!

Appendix VI

TOP 20 FACTORS THAT MAXIMIZE SHAREHOLDER VALUE

Do you know what's important to make your company as valuable as possible?

Successful entrepreneurs know that to maximize long-term shareholder value there's no time like the present! And that means right from your start-up, making sure you keep an eye on the main factors that drive up shareholder value. Exits don't always follow your timetable so you need to move quickly to the 'zone'; the stage you reach when your company is ready to be acquired even if you're not actively looking to sell.

Have a browse through the following top 20 factors and pick out what you think are the five most important.

To get the best value for a small private company on exit, there are many factors that can play a part in getting the best price or deal. Here's my list.

1. A rival bidder – the more the better, and if they know each other, better still. An auction conducted by advisers is best.

2. Gain an insight into the buyer's motivation and needs – the more you know about their business, and which of their needs they're solving by acquiring you, the better you can play up those

attributes of your company. It could be you are in the way of a buyer executing an industry roll-up strategy, who wants to 'bulk up' fast.

3. Get ready to sell – who's taking the lead in negotiations? Are all the 'actors' in the campaign fully briefed? Do you have 'sales collateral' prepared (PPT and business plans plus all financials that make it easy to understand the business)? Are all the company secretarial docs up to date, including monthly CEO reports, etc.? Is there a complete file of customer, supplier and staff contracts gathered together? Appoint an M&A adviser early in the process.

4. Build barriers to entry – it could be your price point for services, your 'must have' technologies, your IP, your dominant market share, your exclusive agreements with leading suppliers or simply a locked-in customer base, but your value will increase if your future revenue is less threatened by new competition.

5. Remember your unique and sustainable market positioning. What do you do that others don't? Why will customers keep coming back to you? Have you ensured your proposition is continually developed ahead of the competition?

6. Operating in a hot sector – like social networking or climate change/renewable energy – but if you don't then find a link, however tenuous, to those hot sectors.

7. Maximize the number of 'blue chip' clients – valuations can double if the bulk of your revenue is with recognized, solidly successful client organizations.

8. A high proportion of contracted and recurring revenues – one-off project revenue is valued lower than recurring revenue because of the repeated cost of customer acquisition, and because it undermines the shareholder value that can be deduced from assured business.

9. Having a credible reason why you want to sell. You must be able to answer the question, 'If you're growing this fast or doing this well, why are you selling, and why now?' Show strength in purpose and don't give any sign of desperation – buyers detect weakness quickly.

10. Commitment to sell – be convincing that you are going to sell to the highest bidder and that you're not testing the market for a valuation.

11. Generating cash at a sufficient level to be entirely self-funding for future growth.

12. High market profile – have you been on the radar of potential buyers for some time? Are you a company that's written or spoken about as being successful and 'one to watch'? Your profile can be enhanced by overt endorsements from major, trusted branded partners or through industry awards.

13. Strong and sustained growth – such that the acquirer can count on continued shareholder value

growth and the NPV (Net Present Value) of that growth can be expressed in present sale price. The more this is evidenced by the forward order book the better.

14. An embedded upside or strategic advantage for buyer. An impressive, credible and content customer base with potential to increase their spend, a management team with capabilities beyond the current organization (ideally already known as individuals to buyer), operating cost savings, intellectual property, geographic presence (implying local know-how).

15. A simple story – a core product/service line that is performing well with no clutter, such as significant (untested) new product lines draining EBITDA (profits) or expensive forays into new markets, including new geographic territories.

16. A revenue model that indicates that the company will become more profitable as it grows – meaning that revenues and gross margins will outgrow the increase in cost of sales and fixed costs.

17. A competent, successful, stable and motivated senior management team – plus a plan for succession in each operational discipline, and/or the ability to reassure the buyer that there can be continuity of key management, if that's what they want.

18. An impressive board and shareholder register with one or more high profile name non-exec directors.

These give the buyer the opportunity to retain the benefit of their contribution, and implicitly lend gravitas to the company by their presence on the board or investor list.

19. Evidence of long-term relationships with professional service providers – banks, lawyers, accountants, etc.

20. No poison pills or factors that will cause transaction delays – such as operating costs (particularly staff costs) out of line with market competition (either under- or overpaid), complex and over-generous options agreements, high accumulated potential redundancy costs, a knot of personal guarantees or agreements that will be expensive or impossible to unwind quickly, litigation, a lack of IP protection (from URLs to registered trademarks to patents) and weak or unsubstantiated data in the due-diligence pack.

NOTES

1 See Jesse Itzler, *Living with a SEAL: 31 Days Training with the Toughest Man on the Planet*, Nashville: Centre Street, 2015

2 Rhett Morris, 'Mentors Are The Secret Weapons of Successful Startups', techcrunch.com, https://techcrunch.com/2015/03/22/mentors-are-the-secret-weapons-of-successful-startups/

3 Professor Mullins's original article is available at https://hbr.org/2013/07/use-customer-cash-to-finance-your-start-up

4 Seedrs campaign advice, Seedrs.com, https://www.seedrs.com/learn/guides/

5 More reading on the layout of an example spreadsheet can be found at: http://smallbusiness.co.uk/profit-and-loss-template-20736/

6 See Carlos Eduardo Espinal, 'How does an early-stage investor value a start-up?'. Full text at http://thedrawingboard.me/2012/01/18/how-does-an-early-stage-investor-value-a-startup/

7 You can find more tips for creating a great PowerPoint presentation from three experts at the following URLS: Carmine Gallo, '10 Questions to Ask When Creating a Killer PowerPoint Presentation', https://www.entrepreneur.com/article/230880; David Larson Levine, '3 Ways Public Humiliation Made Me a Stronger Entrepreneur', https://

www.entrepreneur.com/article/232038; Michael Parker, '25 Pitching Essentials', http://www.pitchcoach.co.uk/slideshare/

8 Seedrs campaign advice, Seedrs.com, https://www.seedrs.com/learn/guides/

9 Scott Volpe, 'Study Shows Business is Better the Second Time Around', dexmedia.com, https://www.dexmedia.com/blog/study-shows-business-better-second-time-around/

10 You can view a list of these codes at https://www.gov.uk/government/uploads/system/uploads/attachment_data/file/455263/SIC_codes_V2.pdf

11 Lucian Camp is a one-man brand, marketing and communications consultant. After a long career in creative agencies, where he began as a copywriter, he now specializes in brand development for service businesses which generally have multiple touch-points with their markets, and which don't provide tangible products

Index

addressable market 38–9, 61–2
Airbnb 20–1, 22
angel investors 4, 12–15, 16, 17–18,
    27, 34, 58, 72, 84, 99, 107, 167
Apple:
  Keynote 65
  Numbers 49
articles of association 97, 139, 146
Artist-Share 2
Artlyst Limited 11
Azalbert, Xavier 93

bank debt 16, 20, 24
barriers to entry, building 172
'blue chip' clients 173
board 135
  chairman 134, 168–9
  directors 13, 42, 101, 139, 140,
    143–4, 145, 164, 167, 168,
    169
  due diligence and 101
  evidence of effectiveness 115
  finance director 134
  investors on 13–15, 97
  management of company 140
  meetings, frequency of 140, 169
  non-executive directors 14, 56,
    115, 134, 167, 168, 169, 174
  payment of 134, 169
  register 174
  shaping a 134, 135, 167–70, 174–5
  shareholder value and 174–5
  size of 134, 167
boatbookings.com 22

brand:
  brand pyramid and defining your
    155–60
  building 136
  core proposition and 44
  domain name and 147–8, 151, 152,
    153, 154
  events and 112
  saying thank you and 122
  selling your story and 79–83
BSB (British Satellite Broadcasting) 20
B2B (Business to Business) 17
Business Connections Live TV 110–11
business continuity 43

Camp, Lucian 82–3, 155–60
campaign, crowdfunding *see* going live
    and under individual campaign
    area
cap table (share history of company)
    49, 72, 97–8
capital gains tax (CGT) 138, 162, 163,
    166
Carillion 2
'carry back' facility, EIS 161, 163
case study: successful crowdfunding
    campaign 27–32
cash flow 9–10, 20–1, 22, 24, 25, 42,
    46, 48, 49, 50–6, 57–60, 61, 130,
    133, 169, 173
chairman 134, 168–9
Cloud Imperium Games 2
communications, donor/
    investor 123–4

Companies House 97, 101, 115, 139,
    140, 142
company, setting up a 97, 142–6
    articles of association 97, 139, 146
    cap table (share history of company)
        49, 72, 97–8
    company secretary 146
    contract of employment, your 97
    corporate directors 143–4
    corporate shareholders 144
    director name(s) 143
    memorandum and articles 146
    office, registered 142–3
    people with significant control
        145–6
    shareholder name(s) 144
    shareholders' agreement 42, 97,
        134, 139–40
    Standard Industry Classification
        (SIC) code 145
    unique company name 142
Crowdcube 25, 28–33, 93, 161–6
crowdfunding:
    alternative funding options 16–34
    campaign 103–20
    case study 27–33
    fees 25–7, 29, 61, 92–3
    financial plan 49–62
    planning campaign 86–102
    preparation for campaign 35–48
    presentation of business to
        investors 63–85
    targets 121–9
    types of 7–15 see also equity
        crowdfunding; crowdlending
        (or debt crowdfunding);
        rewards (or perks)
        crowdfunding
crowdfunding company 1
    advice 32–3
    agreement 91, 92–3
    choosing 29, 78, 87–91
    crowdlending and 8–9
    due diligence see due diligence

extensions 111, 119
failed campaign and 126
fees 25–7, 29, 61, 92–3
functions/role of 91–2
information sent to 72–3
liaising with 113–14
payment from 121–2
staying close to 116
see also under individual company
    name
crowdlending (or debt crowdfunding)
    1, 8–10, 16, 19–20
CrowdShed 11
customer acquisition/selling costs 22,
    53, 76, 117, 122, 173
customer funding 16, 20–4
    deposit model 22
    matchmaker model 21–2
    scarcity model 23–4
    standardize-and-resell model 23
    subscription model 22

debt, bank 24
debt crowdfunding see crowdlending
deposit model 22
determination 2, 4–5, 135
diary, clearing 86–7
directors 13, 42, 101, 139, 140,
    143–4, 145, 164, 167, 168,
    169
discount rate 50
domain name:
    as an asset 154
    associate with what you do 151
    'brandable' 147–8
    choosing 35–6, 147–54
    '.com' 149–50
    creative 152–3
    easy to say 148–9
    infringement risk 150
    keywords 151–2
    length 148
    numbers and punctuation 153
Dropbox 103

due diligence (DD) 11, 30, 32, 73, 97, 100–2, 110, 111, 175

EasyJet 80
EBAN website 99
EIS (Enterprise Investment Scheme) 11, 30, 32, 60, 97, 124, 138, 161–6
  overview 161–2
  restrictions 164
  tax reliefs 162–6
Elevator Pitch 63
email:
  PR, social media and 74–6
  teaser 71–3, 103–4, 106
equity:
  equity crowdfunding 7–8, 10, 12, 16, 18–19, 57–61
  financial plan and 54–5, 56, 57
  how much to give away 57–61, 130, 169
  investment return and 54–5
  pricing 133
  rewards (or perks) crowdfunding and 10–12, 19
Espinal, Carlos Eduardo 60–1
Esso 151
event, launch/mid-campaign 111–13
Excel 49
Exchange Telegraph Company 23
executive summary 64–6, 71–3, 94, 96, 99, 103–4
exit valuation 47
Extel Computing 23
Exxon 151

Facebook 75, 86, 87, 94, 99
fees 14, 25–7, 29, 50, 56, 61, 76, 89, 134, 168, 169
Fiat 500X 42
finance director 134
Financial Conduct Authority (FCA) 30, 60, 94, 100, 107, 124, 125, 137

financial plan 28, 30, 45, 49–62, 64, 72, 96, 125
  cash flow 51–2
  cost of acquisition in relation to lifetime value of customer 53
  cost of sales 50, 53
  discount rate 50
  gross margin 53
  IRR (Internal Rate of Return) per cent 54–5
  operating costs 50, 53, 54
  P/E (price–earnings ratio) 50
  P&L (Profit and Loss) 50, 52
  past trading performance 50
  raising cash/maximum negative cash 53–4
  reducing costs in relation to underperformance 54
  revenue generation 49, 50, 52, 53, 56, 62
  shares given to investors 57–61
  staff costs 50
  underperformance, reacting to 54
  use of funds (justifying the money you want) 55–6
40 per cent rule 4, 5
Friends and Family (F&F) 16, 17, 44, 95, 167
Funding Circle 8
Funding Knight 8

get ready, how to 35–48
  basics, organizing 35–7
  fixing problems 39
  money making 40–2
  plan 40
  problem solving ('market pain') 37–8
  problems with business, possible 42–4
  size of problem 38–9
  team 46–8
  traction 44–6

going live 103–20
   crowdfunding service company
      and 116
   due diligence questions 110
   flagging campaign 119–20
   investors, choosing 114–16
   launch date 111
   launch event/mid-campaign
      event 111–13
   media campaign 117
   nudging an investor into a 'yes'
      decision 108–10
   positive news, feeding 116–17
   potential investors, questions
      from 118–19
   pre-campaign 103–7
   team, organizing 113–14
   webinar 110–11
Google 21, 86, 150, 151–2, 153
   AdWords 36, 44–5, 148
   Alert 4, 117
   Analytics 105
   Docs 103
grants/matched funds 16, 24–5
gross margin 39, 40, 45, 53, 174

H&M 24
Harvard Business Review 21
Hauser, Hermann 62
HMRC 32, 97, 138, 163
hot sector 26, 172
Hyland, Steve 110

income tax relief 11–12, 32, 60, 97,
   138, 161–6
IndieGoGo 2, 25
influencers 74
investors:
   angel 12–15, 16, 17–18, 58, 72, 84,
      99, 167
   choosing 114–16
   list of 93–6
   nudging into a 'yes' decision 108–10
   questions from potential 118–19

   regular communications with 123–4
   tax breaks for *see* tax
Itzler, Jesse 4

Kickstarter 2, 26
KPI charts (Key Performance
   Indicators) 43, 135

launch date 111
launch event/mid-campaign event
   111–13
LawyerFair 64, 110
lawyers/legal fees 8, 30, 44, 47, 61,
   64, 70, 76, 97, 101, 110, 113,
   133, 134, 175
lifetime value, customer 53, 131
LinkedIn 41, 64, 75–6, 94, 99
litigation 30, 44, 133, 175
Logotron 154
London Business School 21, 39
loss relief 12, 163, 166
Low Carbon Innovation Fund 28
Lucian Camp Consulting 155, 156

margins 39, 40, 43, 45, 53–4, 174
market positioning 40–2, 61–2, 172
market profile 173
Marquis Jet 4
matchmaker model 21–2
media campaign 117
memorandum and articles 146
mezzanine selling 106
Microsoft 23, 41, 49, 65, 69
Microventures 2
Monoprix 23–4
Mullins, Professor John 21; *The New
   Business Road Test* 39

name, unique company 142
negative working capital 21
non-executive directors 14, 56, 115,
   134, 167, 168, 169, 174

office, registered 142–3

operating costs 21, 22, 43, 50, 53, 54, 55, 76, 133, 174, 175

P/E (price–earnings ratio) 50
P&L (Profit and Loss) 50, 52
Pebble Watch 2
peer-to-peer lending 8, 100
people with significant control 145–6
picking yourself up, failure and 127–9
pitch 30
    angel clubs and 107
    brand and 81–2
    create a killer 32–3
    'Elevator Pitch' 63
    responding to questions during 33
    website and 83
Pizza Express 151
planning, campaign 86–102
    agreement and fees, negotiating 92–3
    cap table 97–8
    company formation 97
    crowdfunding company, choosing 87–91
    crowdfunding company, role of 91–2
    diary, clearing 86–7
    due diligence and compliance 100–2
    investors you want to approach, list of 93–6, 99
    sales collateral (package of information for investors) 96–7
    social media 99
    website 99–100
Portillo, Michael 161
positive news, feeding 116–17
positive, staying 4–5
PowerPoint 61, 64, 65, 69–71, 72, 96–7
PR 74–6
pre-campaign 15, 18, 30, 77, 92, 97, 100, 101, 103–7, 125 see also get ready, how to
presentation, business 63–85 see also story, how to tell your
Prize: Prezi 65
problem ('market pain'):
    defining 37–8
    fixing 39–40
    size 38–9
Puddick, Daniel 27, 28, 29–30, 31–2

R&D tax credits 25
retiring 126
Reuters News Agency 23
rewards (or perks) crowdfunding 1, 10–12, 16, 19, 77–9, 125
rival bidder 171
Roberts, Chris 2
ROI (return on investment) 49
Ryanair 80

sales:
    collateral (package of information for investors) 71, 96–7, 172
    commitment to sell 173
    concentration on 135
    cost of 44–6, 50, 53
    credible reason to sell 173
    due diligence questions and 110
    getting ready to sell 172
    traction and 44–6
    underperformance 43
scale, building for 134–5
scarcity model 23–4
Seed Enterprise Investment Scheme (SEIS) 32, 60, 97, 138, 161–6
Sellaband 2
SEO (Search Engine Organization) 152
shareholder 42
    agreement 42, 97, 134, 139–40
    name(s) 144
    rights 139–41
    value 171–5

shares, giving away 57–61
short-term promises 123
Small Business, Enterprise and
    Employment Act (2015) 145
    (2016) update 142
social media 37, 68, 74–6, 94, 99,
    106, 110–11, 114, 120, 149
social responsibility 136
staff costs 40, 50, 175 *see also* team
Standard Industry Classification (SIC)
    code 145
standardize-and-resell model 23
Star Citizen (online video game) 2
story, how to tell your 63–85
    branding 79–83
    description of idea and why it will
        work 63–4
    executive summary 65–6, 71–3
    pack of information for
        investors 71–3
    PowerPoint 69–71
    PR, social media and email
        messages 74–6
    rewards, listing and pricing 77–9
    team 83–4
    teaser email 71–3
    video 67–9, 73–4
    visuals and graphics 79
    website 83
subscription documents 72
subscription model 22
success, secrets of 130–2
successful crowdfunding campaign
    (case study) 27–33
Sundried 12, 27–32

targets 121–9
    communications with donors/
        investors 123–4
    failing to hit target 124–9
        learning from what went
            wrong 126–7
        picking yourself up 127–9
        retiring gracefully 126

topping up funding yourself
    124–5
money into bank account, getting
    the 121–2
reaching your target 121
short-term promises, delivering
    123
thank you, saying 122
tax:
    R&D tax credits 16, 25
    relief, SEIS and EIS 11–12, 32, 60,
        97, 138, 161–6
team 32, 35, 36, 38, 43, 174
    choosing and rewarding 35, 36, 56,
        83–4, 135
    costs/salaries 40, 50, 56, 175
    impressing investors and 46–8
    organizing 113–14
    problems with 43, 84, 128, 133
    telling your story and 61, 66, 81–2
    weak members 84, 128, 133
    see also board
teaser email 71–3, 103, 106
thank you, saying 122
Thin Cats 8
top up, funding 124–5
traction 20, 37, 44–6, 61, 62, 66, 76,
    81, 103, 104, 130
trading performance, tracking 43, 50
Twitter 64, 75, 94, 99

Uber 41–2
US Navy SEAL 4, 5

valuation, company 10, 20, 27–8, 46,
    47, 50, 57–61, 134, 154, 173
venture capital (VC) 17, 20, 27, 28,
    32, 62, 132, 163, 167
video 30, 61, 64–74, 89, 111, 112, 127
    scripting, shooting and
        editing 73–4, 89
    six tips for getting it right 67–9
visual media 65
visuals and graphics 79

Volpe, Scott, 'Study Shows Business is
    Better The Second Time Around'
    (article) 127

Warburg, Mike 23
webinar 65, 110–11

website 17, 44–5, 72, 83, 99–100,
    105, 152 *see also* domain name

Xing 41

Zara 23